The Chinese Community in Toronto

The
CHINESE COMMUNITY
in Toronto

Then and Now

by Arlene Chan

DUNDURN
TORONTO

Project Editor: Britanie Wilson
Editor: Dominic Farrell
Design: Courtney Horner

Library and Archives Canada Cataloguing in Publication

Chan, Arlene
The Chinese community in Toronto : then and now / Arlene Chan.

Includes bibliographical references and index.
Issued also in electronic formats.
ISBN 978-1-4597-0769-6

1. Chinese Canadians--Ontario--Toronto--History. 2. Chinatown
(Toronto, Ont.)--History. 3. Toronto (Ont.)--Ethnic relations--History.
I. Title.

FC3097.9.C5C49 2013   971.3'541004951   C2013-900772-5

1   2   3   4   5   17   16   15   14   13

| Conseil des Arts du Canada / Canada Council for the Arts | Canada | ONTARIO ARTS COUNCIL / CONSEIL DES ARTS DE L'ONTARIO |

We acknowledge the support of the **Canada Council for the Arts** and the **Ontario Arts Council** for our publishing program. We also acknowledge the financial support of the **Government of Canada** through the **Canada Book Fund** and **Livres Canada Books**, and the **Government of Ontario** through the **Ontario Book Publishing Tax Credit** and the **Ontario Media Development Corporation**.

VISIT US AT
Dundurn.com | Definingcanada.ca | @dundurnpress | Facebook.com/dundurnpress

Dundurn
3 Church Street, Suite 500
Toronto, Ontario, Canada
M5E 1M2

Front cover images:
Chinatown's mural. Jens Ronneberger, Chi Ping Dance Company, Chinese Temple. Tam Kam Chiu, Dragon boat race. Tam Kam Chiu.
Back cover image:
Chinatown's Gateway, William Greer.

Dedicated to my granddaughter, Audrey,
and all the other children whose lives have been enriched by our collective past.

Contents

Acknowledgements | 9

Introduction | 11

1 | Gold Mountain and the Canadian Pacific Railway, 1858–1885 | 13

2 | Early Settlement in Toronto, 1878–1922 | 33

3 | Living in Chinatown | 45

4 | A Child's Life | 63

5 | The War Years | 71

6 | Post-War Years | 85

7 | Toronto's Chinatowns | 103

8 | A Diverse Community | 123

9 | Noted Toronto Chinese | 139

Appendix A | 153
Chinese Canadians Appointed Member of the Order of Canada, 1976–2011
(Greater Toronto Area)

Appendix B | 155
Chinese Canadians Appointed to the Order of Ontario, 1991–2011
(Greater Toronto Area)

Chronology | 157

Notes | 161

Glossary | 167

Further Reading | 171

Index | 175

Acknowledgements

My deepest gratitude is extended to Kirk Howard and the others at Dundurn Press, especially Barry Penhale and Jane Gibson, who have nurtured my long-standing passion for Chinese-Canadian history and given me another opportunity to tell the stories of the Chinese in Toronto.

I praise the dedication of archivists and librarians of Library and Archives Canada, the City of Toronto Archives, the Toronto Public Library, the Multicultural History Society of Ontario, and the Vancouver Public Library for preserving our past and making it so accessible.

I would be remiss not to acknowledge a cast of others who assisted in my earlier book, *The Chinese in Toronto from 1878*.

The images make the stories come alive, and so I would like to give special thanks to Jens Ronneberger and Tam Kam Chiu for their photographs, my son Michael Chan for his maps, and Emily Chou, my first cousin once removed, for her graphic illustration. Victor and Nelson Wong, Jim Rosenthal, Roberta Lau, Keith Lock, and Mavis Garland have my deepest appreciation for opening up their treasured family albums. My gratitude to Andrea Yermy, Mary Anne Wilson, and Emily Fong for keeping my manuscript on track, and to Dominic Farrell for his razor-sharp editing.

I thank Henry Kelsey Senior Public School, Principal Lucie Lepage, and School Trustee Shaun Chen for introducing me to a wonderful group of Grade 8 students, who guided me during the early phase of writing the manuscript. Thank you Faiza, William, Kajan, Elim, Angela, and Gayathri.

Last but not least, I add my gratitude to Leo and my family who have supported me, as always, from start to finish.

Introduction

This book is about the Chinese in Toronto and their stories. It is about immigrants who have come not only from China, but from around the globe, and brought with them the determination and courage to start a new life despite all odds. For over one hundred years, their contribution has been a vital part of the cultural and social diversity that makes Toronto one of the most multicultural cities in the world.

Aside from the First Nations peoples, we are all immigrants or descendants of immigrants. All Torontonians, whatever their origin, have a story to tell of how someone in their family came to the city.

Some arrived only yesterday; others landed generations earlier. My grandfather arrived from Taishan, Guangdong province, in 1899, and brought over my grandmother a few years later — both had to pay the head tax. They raised their twelve children — my mother, Jean, among them — in Nanaimo, then Vancouver, British Columbia. She moved to Toronto when she was sixteen years old to earn money to help her family through the Depression. My father, Doyle Lumb, came from Xinhui, Guangdong province, as a twelve-year-old in 1921. He met my mother through a matchmaker and they married in 1939. Their first business together was a grocery store; then they ran the Kwong Chow Restaurant in Chinatown. Both of them were very active in the Chinese community — so much so that my mother was the first Chinese-Canadian woman to receive the Order of Canada, our country's highest civilian honour.

My five brothers and sisters and I were born in Toronto. I grew up in Chinatown where I attended Ogden and Ryerson

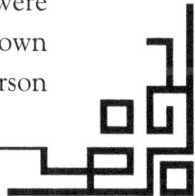

schools, as well as Chinese school at the Chinese Presbyterian Church on Beverley Street. Because of my parents, I spent a lot of time in Chinatown: attending events organized by the Lem Family Association, working at my parents' restaurant, watching Chinese movies at the Casino on Queen Street, eating at Chinese banquets, and learning Chinese folk and classical dances. As I did my research on the Chinese in Toronto, so many happy memories flooded back — memories filled with faces and places from my childhood years.

Those memories are a personal treasure; similar ones are a common legacy shared by others in the Chinese community in Toronto. Some time ago, however, I came to the harsh realization that outside the Chinese community little was known about the story of the Chinese in Canada and Toronto. Stories about Chinese Canadians have not been told in books, on television, or in newspapers and magazines. Very few Canadians know about their important contribution because their stories have been kept within the family or silenced as too painful a secret to share. There's an old expression: A country that does not remember its past has no future. We need to look to the past to move forward.

Chinese Canadians have added to the rich fabric of Canadian life in so many ways. Each wave of Chinese immigrants has been unique. The early immigrants were the most homogeneous — most of them came from southern China, spoke the same language, and shared the same culture and traditions. Since World War Two, however, the makeup of the Chinese immigrants coming to Canada has changed significantly. Those arriving today come from many different places, and they bring with them a diversity of backgrounds in education, skills, financial well-being, and ethnicity. From artists and dancers to activists and military heroes, Chinese Canadians are proud to let everyone know about their contribution, then and now.

ONE

Gold Mountain and the Canadian Pacific Railway, 1858–1885

The story of the Chinese in Toronto begins in China, the third largest country and the oldest surviving civilization in the world. While its origins date back five thousand years, China today is a modern country with a rich and varied culture. It is also an economic giant, one that has a huge population, as well. Indeed, China has a population today of over 1.3 billion people, that is, one in five of the world's population. The largest ethnic group by far is the Han Chinese, who make up more than 90 percent of China's population, while no less than fifty-six minority groups make up the balance.

The Chinese name for China is "Zhongguo," which means *Middle Kingdom*. For a long time, the Chinese believed that their country was the centre of the civilized world. They had good reason for believing this. In earlier times China was envied as a rich and powerful country, one with the most advanced science and technology. It had a flourishing culture where literature, music, and other arts thrived. The Chinese were the first to develop papermaking and printing. Gun powder was invented for spectacular fireworks, rockets, and weapons. Among many other early inventions were a magnetic compass and the first seismoscope or earthquake-detection machine.

Despite the country's impressive cultural and scientific legacy, most people were farmers, who lived simple lives, eating the rice that they had planted. Rarely travelling beyond their villages, they worked the land, handed down from generation to generation, or they farmed for landowners who claimed a share of their crops as rent. In the fall the whole family, children included, harvested the crops.

Just as China has a long and storied history, its contact with the West also goes back a long time. Most are familiar with Marco Polo's trips to China in the late thirteenth century, but there is evidence that Buddhist monks travelled to the shores of North America long before that — nearly one thousand years earlier, in the fifth century. The first official record of the Chinese landing on what is now Canada's west coast, however, documents a group of fifty labourers, carpenters, and ship-builders. They set sail aboard the ship *Felice* from Macau with Captain John Meares in 1788. Vancouver Island was the landing point; there, a trading post for sea otter pelts was built. These were in high demand in China for belts, capes, and robes because the fur was highly prized by the wealthy there.

• • •

Half-Belly

It was not until the mid-1800s that the Chinese began leaving China in great numbers, though. The country's population had doubled, and overcrowding caused shortages of land to feed its 420 million people. Poverty and starvation resulted in deaths, and this dire situation was especially true in the province of Guangdong in the most southerly part of China (see map of China). As well as suffering from a shortage of land, the area had been devastated by a series of natural disasters. Indeed, in one small area of the Pearl River Delta, between 1852 and 1908, there were fourteen floods, seven typhoons, four earthquakes, two droughts, four plagues, and five famines.[1] As a result there was barely enough food to feed one-third of its people, twenty-eight million in 1850.

Profile

"I discovered that my grandfather was not a landlord but an extremely poor peasant who starved most of the time. They said his nick-name was 'Half-Belly,' meaning that his stomach was never full."[2]

~ Jan Wong, Toronto author and journalist.

Not only were there natural disasters to bear, the poor peasants had to pay high taxes. If farm crops failed because of bad weather, money was borrowed to pay the taxes. It might take years to pay back this loan because

CHINA

GUANGDONG

Michael Chan.

Most of the early immigrants came from the province of Guangdong in southern China.

moneylenders charged high interest rates. Some farmers became bandits, who raided farm villages for food in order to stay alive. Peasant rebellions against the government added havoc and claimed hundreds of thousands of lives. The situation was desperate. Then stories started spreading in the villages, stories about a faraway place where one could get rich. What could have been more welcome! This unknown land glittered with gold; the place was called *Gum Shan*, or "Gold Mountain."

Did You Know?

Gold Mountain is a translation of *Gum Shan*; the Chinese name refers to the gold that was discovered in North America, first in California, then in British Columbia. Gold Mountain was the land of dreams.

• • •

Gold Rush

Gold was discovered in 1858 in the Fraser River of British Columbia. Usually, gold has to be mined with expensive equipment to extract it from the veins of the rocks. In the Fraser River, however, earthquakes, glaciers, and floods had released the gold from the rocks, and as a result the gold could be found in the river's flowing waters. Sometimes this precious metal was found in the shape of nuggets. More often it was present in flakes or fine dust. With no fancy equipment required, miners used a simple pan, scooped the gravel and sand from the river, and swirled it around in search of gold.

Although the earliest Chinese prospectors in the Fraser River valley came from California, where the gold rush had come to an end, thousands more soon followed from China. Of all those seeking gold, the most conspicuous were the Chinese. They spoke a totally different language, they ate with chopsticks, they wore odd-looking jackets with cloth buttons. Even their shoes were made out of cloth. The strangest thing of all was the fact that they wore their hair long; not only was their hair black and long, it was tied back in a braid, or *queue*. This hairstyle was mandatory in China. Any man who cut off his braid was executed for the crime of treason against the government. Whenever pranksters in North America yanked on a Chinese man's queue,

Library and Archives Canada/PA-125990.

Chinese gold miners, like this one panning for gold on the Fraser River in 1875, only dared to rework sites abandoned by white miners; otherwise, they'd be beaten and robbed.

or worse yet, cut it off, these acts of bullying caused great shame. All of these differences made the Chinese stand out. They were frequently singled out, beaten up, and robbed.

Even Canadian policemen were known to tie men together by their queues.[3]

By the end of the gold rush, in the mid-1860s, only a handful of Chinese had realized

Library and Archives Canada/C-50449.

This *Canadian Illustrated News* cartoon from October 15, 1870, shows Americans grabbing a man's queue and beating him with their sticks.

their dreams of getting rich. Some had earned a bit, but the vast majority found little to no gold. Life in Gold Mountain was not what they had expected and many returned home to China empty-handed.

• • •

Canadian Pacific Railway

The second wave of Chinese immigrants came to build the Canadian Pacific Railway. As a means of persuading British Columbia to become a part of Canada, Prime Minister John A. Macdonald promised a railway to connect British Columbia with the eastern provinces. British Columbia agreed and Canada gained its sixth province in 1871.

It was estimated by Andrew Onderdonk, the American contractor hired to oversee the building of the railway, that a workforce of ten thousand labourers would be needed. There weren't enough local workers to do the job, however; in fact, there were no more than about four hundred of them available. As a result Onderdonk recommended that workers be imported from China.

The Chinese had a good reputation as capable and reliable labourers. They had been hired to build railways in the United States, where they not only worked hard but did so for lower wages than other workers. Hiring Chinese workers would allow the railway to be built at a cheaper cost, one within its budget. As a clincher for his proposal, Onderdonk argued that a race of people that could build the Great Wall of China could easily construct a railway.[4]

When Onderdonk announced his plan for importing Chinese labourers, the people of British Columbia responded angrily. They weren't happy about the Chinese coming and taking jobs from Canadians, and their opposition was strongly supported by the media. The *Mainland Guardian*, for example, reported, "Chinese competition unequal, immoral and vicious."[5]

In defence of hiring the Chinese, Prime Minister Macdonald said, "Either you must have this labour or you cannot have the railway."[6] Although white Canadians objected, failure to fulfill the promise of a railway was not an option. In the end seventeen thousand Chinese labourers were hired.

• • •

Big-Eyed Roosters

Railway representatives travelled to China to recruit workers, encouraging suitable candidates to leave the misery of their villages and come to Canada to make lots of money. The long lineups of those looking to sign up for work were mostly made up of young males, between the ages of eighteen and forty. There were boys, too, some as young as twelve, who lied about their age. That's how desperate they were to get a job. They usually ended up working as tea-boys, serving Chinese tea to the workers and helping the cooks prepare meals.

Most recruits were poor peasants from the province of Guangdong who borrowed money and sold off their meagre possessions to buy the ship fare. Those unable to collect enough money signed contracts promising to pay back the money for their fare out of their wages. Since they didn't know how to write, they pressed their fingerprints on the work contracts. The words, read out in a loud voice by the translator, told them they had jobs and that their pay would be deducted every month until they'd paid back their ship fare. It was a big risk to sign up, but wasn't it worth it in order to search for a better life?

With a few belongings wrapped in a cloth bundle, the men boarded the ships. The early ones were small, three-masted sailing vessels that became known as "big-eyed roosters" because the ships' bows looked like rooster heads, with huge, bulging eyes.

The trip across the Pacific Ocean from China to Canada took up to several months. As Goon Ling Dang remembered, "I came over on a sailing ship; we were fifty-six days on the trip; just a small sailing vessel about two hundred feet long."[7]

People were packed like sardines, crammed on the floor, shoulder to shoulder, knee to knee, and locked in steerage, the bottom part of the ship. Even though there were no windows or ventilation, they were

Profile

Sam Eng, who became a well-respected elder in Toronto's Chinese community, came to Canada at the age of thirteen. He remembered the voyage: "I felt sick … seasick. I'd never been in a boat before in China and I had to go through the Pacific Ocean.... The ship was so small the waves almost came over. You rolled on the boat just like a rocking chair."[8]

Vancouver Public Library, Pl. 12866.

These young men are on a ship bound for Canada.

only allowed to come on deck for fresh air a few times each day. No one could bathe and many were seasick. The stale air was shared among hundreds of strangers who suffered in misery during the long voyage.

With no fresh fruit and vegetables, many became ill with scurvy, a disease caused by the lack of Vitamin C. Starvation took the lives of those who relied on eating the ship's daily ration of tea and rice. No one had told them to bring their own supply of dried meats and vegetables. Bodies were dumped overboard into the ocean.

• • •

A Dollar A Day

The ship excursion was only the beginning of a life of hardship for the new Chinese immigrants. Things went from bad to worse when they reported for work in Canada. Twelve hours a day, six days a week, the Chinese workers were assigned backbreaking tasks: cutting through rocks, moving heavy boulders, building bridges, and chopping down trees. They used sledgehammers, chisels, and axes to chip away at the Rocky Mountains, but even with these tools, it was hard work getting the job done.

The railway construction through British Columbia had particular challenges. It was necessary to carve a route through the mountainous terrain; the workers also had to build enormous bridges to span the vast canyons of the Thompson and Fraser rivers. Accomplishing these feats required engineering ingenuity and the labour of many men, toiling in dangerous working conditions and, often, taking life-threatening risks.

One way to tunnel through the mountains was with nitroglycerine, a highly explosive liquid. It is less expensive than dynamite but also more unpredictable. In fact, it is so unstable that the slightest movement can cause it to detonate spontaneously. The builders of the railway decided to use it anyway, although there was a risk of killing, seriously maiming, or burying men alive in landslides if the liquid exploded unexpectedly.

In 1880 nine Chinese were killed or seriously injured in a blast. According to Chinese witnesses, no warning had been sounded by the white foreman. He claimed that a warning had been given, but the Chinese didn't understand him.[9] In the same year, another accident killed two Chinese men when a rock rolled onto one man and a larger rock caused the second one to fall down a cliff.[10]

Borne & May/Library and Archives Canada/C-006686B.

Labourers are shown in 1884 working on the construction of the Canadian Pacific Railway.

Deaths from nitroglycerin accidents, as well as overwork, collapsing bridges, disease, exposure to cold weather, illness, and malnutrition were not uncommon. One man recalled his father's stories about the severe weather conditions: "My father … was not prepared for the cold winters in Canada, nor were any other of the Chinese. They arrived in their thin clothing, cloth shoes, still wearing their pigtails, and the railway did not provide them with gloves, hats, or any kind of work clothing. When the winter snows came, they still worked in their cloth shoes, and my father told me that he had to wrap burlap sacks around his feet to keep from freezing."[11]

Although other deaths were generally not recorded, it is estimated that at least one Chinese died for every mile of railway track laid.

What amount of pay would have been fair wage for such perilous work? The Chinese received a dollar a day, half of what white workers were paid. In a month they earned twenty-five dollars, which they then spent on supplies, clothing, rent, tools, taxes, medicine, oil, and tobacco.[12] There was little left after paying for these living and working expenses.

• • •

From Sea To Sea

In 1885 the Canadian Pacific Railway was completed. The driving of the "Last Spike" at Craigellachie, British Columbia, took place on the cold morning of November 7 at 9:22 a.m. This historical event was attended by a crowd of politicians and other dignitaries. Donald Alexander Smith, a Canadian Pacific Railway director, raised and struck his hammer, driving in the last iron spike — the greatest symbolic act of Canada's national unity. The transcontinental railway, the backbone of the nation and the greatest engineering feat of its day, now joined the country "from sea to sea," as in Canada's national motto *A Mari Usque Ad Mare*.

Did You Know?

Singer and songwriter Gordon Lightfoot composed the "Canadian Railroad Trilogy" to commemorate the railway workers on the occasion of Canada's Centennial in 1967. The words of the six-minute song were later used to create a picture book, illustrated by Canadian artist Ian Wallace.

Not one Chinese labourer was invited to the ceremony, even though three-quarters of the railway workers were Chinese. Their contribution to nation-building ended up going unrecorded in the history books, until the Canadian government officially recognized their hard work and sacrifice almost one hundred years later. In 1980 Parliament passed a motion to acknowledge "the contribution made to the Canadian mosaic and culture by the people of Chinese background."

• • •

Jean Lumb Collection.

The Memorial to Commemorate the Chinese Railroad Workers in Canada is located near the train tracks and Union Station and at the foot of Rogers Centre in Toronto.

We Are Hated

Once the Canadian Pacific Railway was completed, thousands of workers were laid off. They no longer had jobs. Nor could they find others. The economy was on the verge of a depression, and there was little work to be found. The Chinese were made into scapegoats, blamed for all of British Columbia's economic and social problems. Canadians really didn't want the Chinese to stay and they certainly didn't want any more coming into Canada.

Jobs were in short supply and the level of competition for work was fierce. White Canadians claimed that the Chinese had an unfair advantage because they worked for lower wages. Pointing out their squalid living conditions and absence of families, white workers argued that the Chinese also didn't need as much money for their daily living expenses. With so few jobs, the whites argued, it was unfair that the Chinese were being employed while white Canadians were out of work.

Anti-Chinese discrimination broke out as Canadians from all walks of life demanded that the Chinese leave the country. Almost one thousand Chinese went back to China; more might have left if Andrew Onderdonk had kept his promise of providing a return ticket back to China. However, that promise was never honoured, and so many of the Chinese labourers who had worked so hard to build the CPR remained in Canada. For the majority who stayed, there was a constant battle against fierce discrimination. As one man remembered, "We know we are not welcomed in Canada. We are hated. But we have to make a living. We have a family to support in China.... We are just hated by the whites."[13]

The *Port Moody Gazette* reported: "Would it not, therefore, be a wise scheme for our local Government to charter a few vessels and send the Chinese back to their native land, free. We believe very many of them would readily avail themselves of such an opportunity, now that work is scarce, and furthermore, that to return is the aspiration, if not the destination, of nearly every Chinaman in the country."[14]

• • •

White Canada

Politicians were no less vocal about their anti-Chinese sentiments. The Conservative Party campaigned in British Columbia for a "White Canada" and "the absolute exclusion of Asiatics." The Liberal Party shared the same campaign platform, claiming "that Canada should remain a white man's country."[15]

Since Canada's Confederation in 1867, the government had clearly encouraged newcomers to come and settle, especially in the Prairies; however, only immigrants who were white, that is those of British and European heritage, were recruited. Pamphlets advertising free land attracted over 650,000 settlers, who arrived from Scandinavia, Germany, Russia, Ukraine, Poland, Romania, and Austria-Hungary.

WHITE IMMIGRATION · ORIENTAL EXCLUSION

B.C. IMMIGRATION POLICY

THE SAME ACT WHICH EXCLUDES ORIENTALS SHOULD OPEN WIDE THE PORTALS OF BRITISH COLUMBIA TO WHITE IMMIGRATION.

A 1907 political cartoon shows a gate closed to Chinese men while the gatekeeper, a woman wearing a dress made out of a Union Jack, welcomes well-dressed, white immigrants with their families.

Vancouver Public Library, 39046.

The door into Canada was not open to the Chinese; they certainly did not fit the vision for a white Canada. As much as the government's position was a reflection of the times, it was nonetheless racist.

• • •

Silks, Teas, and Opium

To understand why there was such anti-Chinese discrimination, one has to look at what was also happening around the world. The most powerful person in the world at the time was Queen Victoria, who reigned for sixty-four years, from 1837 until 1901, as the ruler of the British Empire. Her vast empire included Canada, India, Australia, New Zealand, and large parts of Africa.

China was rich with silks, teas, and fine goods, and these products were highly valued by European countries. Chinese rulers had long been wary of Westerners, however, and as early as the Ming dynasty (1368–1644), they had limited foreign trade in China. During the Qing dynasty (1644–1911), foreigners were treated with the same caution. China only allowed them to trade and settle in certain port cities, Hong Kong and Macau being the most popular.

When European traders started to spread into the interior, China tried to stop them. However, Western armies and navies retaliated with superior force, and the once powerful Chinese empire began to crumble. The country had long viewed itself as the centre of the world, but following the loss of the Opium Wars (a name for two wars between England and China), its glory faded. The loss also marked the beginning of the end for the Qing dynasty. Foreign governments of Britain, Germany, France, and Russia occupied parts of China and imposed restrictions on its people. China was now regarded by Western countries as weak, so when the Chinese went overseas as labourers, they were regarded as inferiors and treated with disrespect and discrimination.

• • •

Head Tax

Canadians showed their objections to the Chinese with protests and riots. Politicians at all levels of government voiced their anti-Chinese sentiments. There was tremendous pressure for a solution to the "Chinese question." In response the Canadian government introduced an entry fee, a head tax of fifty dollars, in 1885. All Chinese coming into the country were forced to pay this head tax, an amount that was intended to be a financial hardship and a deterrent to further Chinese immigration.

Did You Know?

The Canadian government appointed a Royal Commission, a public enquiry, to study the "Chinese question." The report concluded that the Chinese were "perpetual foreigners" who were taking work away from white workers. It also noted that the average Chinese worker in Canada earned $225 a year and his savings amounted to $43, after paying for rent, medicine, clothing, and food. Based on this finding, the head tax that was recommended by the report was set at fifty dollars to make the entry fee too expensive for the average Chinese worker.

The government underestimated how desperately the Chinese wanted to leave China; they kept coming to Canada, despite the head tax. The political and economic conditions in China were worse than ever. Chinese labourers could only earn two dollars a month in China, whereas in Canada they could earn ten to twenty times more. Friends and relatives pooled their money to pay the passage for someone from their village, who, once he was working in Canada, would send money home. As David Chu remembered, "If you looked at our village, our ancestral village ... it was our ticket out of poverty, out of the Third World."[16] Gim Wong remembered how his uncle had been sent over: "Villages did everything they could to send one person over, in hopes he would do what he could to help the village."[17]

The government raised the head tax to one hundred dollars in 1900, then five hundred dollars in 1903. Five hundred dollars was worth two years' wages, enough to buy two houses. This tax was very expensive, not only for the men who wanted to come but for anyone who was already in Canada and had the dream of bringing his wife and children over. That was the intent of the government: to prevent family life in Canada and discourage the growth of the Chinese population. No other immigrant group had to pay such a tax to enter the country.

Doug Chin Collection.

This head tax certificate shows that Chin Ng (Chin Ng Jai) arrived in Vancouver on March 3, 1918, and paid the five hundred dollar head tax.

Library and Archives Canada/PA-118185.

This family is en route to Canada aboard the *Black Diamond* in 1889. Based on his Western attire, this man was likely a wealthy merchant who could afford to pay the fifty dollar head tax for his wife, mother, and four children.

Profile

In 1921 Doyle Lumb was twelve years old. That year he crossed the Pacific Ocean on the *Empress of Russia*. After one month of voyage, the ship docked at Vancouver, where he had to stay in a prison-like detention house by the dock and wait to be processed by the immigration authorities. He considered himself lucky, because his stay there was only one month; others were locked up there for a much longer time. After he passed inspection, his father, who had awaited his son's release, paid the five hundred dollar head tax for entry into Canada.

• • •

Not Wanted

The head tax was not the sole anti-Chinese legislation passed in British Columbia. Between 1878 and 1899, twenty-six laws were passed to prevent or restrict the rights of the Chinese. These included laws forbidding voting rights, purchase of Crown (government) land, and employment in the construction of roads, bridges, and other public works. More restrictions were later introduced for the Chinese, such as segregation in restaurants and movie theatres, a ban from public swimming pools, and a law preventing the hiring of white women in Chinese restaurants and laundries.

Not wanted, the Chinese left British Columbia in great numbers. They hopped on the train to travel east to the Prairies, Ontario, and the Maritimes — on the very railway they had built to unite the nation. Whenever the train stopped at a small town, a few would get off to look for work. Although they took whatever jobs that they could find, most ended up running restaurants and laundries in the small towns the train travelled through. That is why there were so many of these businesses all across Canada along the train route.

TWO

Early Settlement in Toronto, 1878–1922

By the late 1800s, Toronto was growing by leaps and bounds, and was well on its way to becoming a major urban centre. Newcomers from England, Scotland, Ireland, Germany, and Italy poured into the city. This growth was largely due to the railway that linked Toronto with everywhere else in Canada. New factories sprang up to serve the rail industry, and new businesses to serve the factories.

The first Chinese man known to have become a resident of Toronto was Sam Ching, who was recorded in the city directory of 1878. He owned a laundry at 9 Adelaide Street East, close to the railway station. Soon other Chinese moved into the city. In the 1881 census, there were ten Chinese, and by 1891 there were thirty-three. Like Sam Ching most of them worked in laundries. At this time a new city hall, now called "Old City Hall," was being built.

By 1915 a small cluster of Chinese businesses and residences were established on York Street; this community then expanded along Queen Street West and up Elizabeth Street.

Why did most Chinese end up living in the same area? One reason was that the

Faces, including some Chinese ones, are carved in stone at the top of the pillars at Old City Hall.

Jean Lumb Collection.

Edouard Deville/Library and Archives Canada/C-021990.

This photo from 1886 shows a tent camp located beside the railway tracks where the Chinese were segregated from the other workers.

Chinese, like most other immigrant groups, wanted to be with others who shared the same language and customs. Another reason for staying together was that the Chinese were not welcome elsewhere. They could not live and work wherever they wanted. When the early Chinese worked on the railway in British Columbia, their tents were pitched beside the train tracks but apart from the white workers. If they lived in towns such as Victoria and Barkerville, the only places they could rent were in the poorest sections, again far away from the white residents. In Toronto, as in each of the other towns where they were found, this cluster of Chinese homes and businesses became known as Chinatown.

Did You Know?

The Tang Dynasty (618–907) is regarded by some historians as the golden age of Chinese civilization, when politics, economics, and military power flourished alongside literature, art, and poetry. To this day the Chinese still refer to themselves as Tang people.

The origin of the term "Chinatown" is unknown. Other labels for such areas, such as "the Chinese quarter" and "the Chinamen's quarter," were commonly used in the early years. The labelling of an area as "Chinatown" may have been a way for white society to keep the Chinese segregated. Or, the term might have evolved from what the Chinese refer to as *Tangrenjie*, literally translated as "street of the Tang people." Whatever the origin, Chinatown is an internationally recognized name for a Chinese area.

• • •

The Ward

In Toronto the area where the early Chinese lived was no different from their settlements in British Columbia and across Canada — the poorest part of town, close to the railway station, and segregated from the white community. The worst slum area in the city, known as "The Ward," was heavily populated by the poorest immigrants. The first people to live there were the Irish, Italians, and East European Jews. They were all fugitives — the Italians and Irish from famine, and the Jews from persecution in Hungary, Poland, and Russia.

Three quarters of the houses in The Ward had no indoor plumbing, and the outdoor toilets were overused by the dozens who shared them. While some streets were paved with cedar blocks, most were just plain mud, and were strewn with smelly and rotting garbage, quite literally thrown out the front door in the days before trash collection.

The Ward cottages were built in the laneways, like this one at the rear of 21 Elizabeth Street, so that landlords could squeeze in more renters and make more money.

Adding to the mess was the manure that could be found everywhere on the roads. Horse-drawn vehicles were the main means of transportation at this time, and horse droppings were a fact of life in the city. The city's street sweepers did scoop and deposit the droppings into garbage cans handily outfitted with wheels, but between their rounds the streets were fouled with manure.

Did You Know?

In its early days, Toronto was divided into five wards, or sections: St. Andrew's, St. George's, St. Patrick's, St. David's, and St. Lawrence's. By 1891 the city had grown and the number of wards had grown, too, increasing from five to thirteen. At that time the city replaced the names of the wards with numbers: Ward 1, Ward 2, Ward 3, et cetera. The boundary of "The Ward," formerly called St. John's Ward, was Yonge Street, University Avenue, College Street, and Queen Street.

The conditions inside were no better. The fortunate few had enough money in the winter to heat their homes with coal, but most bundled up in as many layers of clothing as possible to keep warm. For the poor there was usually little food, too. As a result disease and poverty were so prevalent that the city's first poor house was opened on Elm Street to help impoverished and unemployed people.

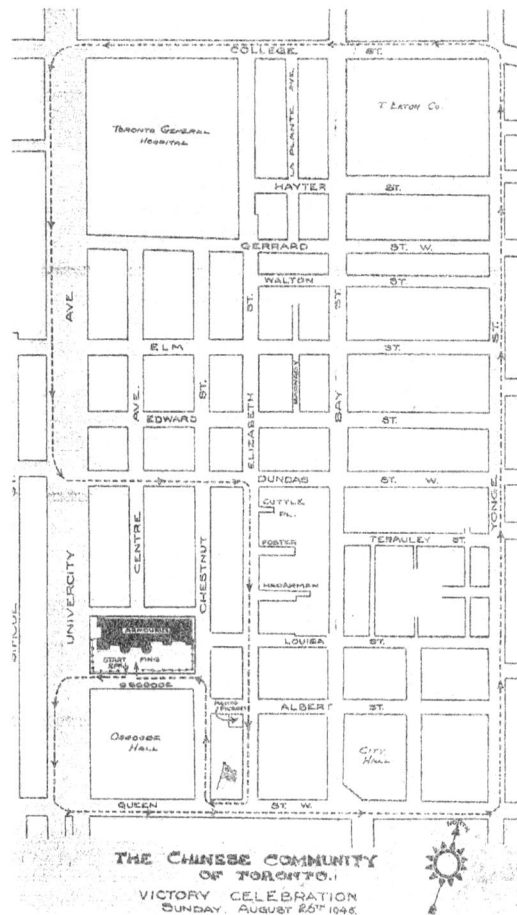

This map, which shows the boundaries of the Ward and the location of Chinatown, outlines the route of a parade organized by the Chinese community to celebrate VJ Day.

Toronto Archives, Fonds 200, Series 372, Sub-series 33, Item 160.

A Chinatown street scene at 83–91 Elizabeth Street in 1937 shows typical one- and two-storey buildings, with stores on the first floor and living quarters on the second floor.

By 1911 more than ten thousand people lived in The Ward. Of these, 70 percent were Jewish. Elizabeth, Elm, and Edward Streets were jammed with small shops, restaurants, and rows of broken-down shacks. Eventually, most of the original inhabitants of The Ward moved out, partly because the city had expro-priated much of the land in the area to build the General Hospital and the Land Registry; partly because of the lure of more prosperous areas of the city. As the Italians moved away to Little Italy around College and Grace Streets, and the Jews to Spadina Avenue, the Chinese moved into The Ward.

Even though less than 1 percent of Toronto's population was Chinese, there was a lot of discrimination. The media played no small part in spreading discriminatory opinions about the "Asiatic" and "Yellow" peril. Headlines and news in national magazines and Toronto's local newspapers show the low regard for the city's Chinese:

- "The Evil the Chinese Do" — *Toronto Star*, 1894;
- "This is a white man's country and white men will keep it so" — *Saturday Night*, 1906;
- "Asiatic Peril to National Life" — *Globe* 1907;
- "One need only … notice the throngs of Chinese lounging in the streets and doorways to realize that the 'Yellow Peril' is more than a mere word in this city" — *Jack Canuck*, 1911;
- "Ching Chang Chinaman, Muchee, Muchee Glad" — *Toronto Star*, 1922.

• • •

No Ticket, No Laundry

The early Chinese worked in laundries. Why was this such a popular business among the Chinese? First, there was a huge demand from people who needed to have their clothes washed and ironed. There were no washers and dryers in those days. Second, no one else wanted to go into the laundry business. It was normal for those running laundries to work sixteen to eighteen hours a day, six to seven days a week. Despite the long hours and hard work, not much money was earned. Third, the Chinese could open a laundry with little money, inexpensive equipment, and simple supplies. Rent money was saved by living at the back of the laundry. Not only that, they could be their own bosses, hire their relatives and friends, and not have to worry about discrimination from white employers. With no training, education, or command of the English language, the Chinese found a niche business.

Most of their customers were non-Chinese. Many Chinese laundrymen did not know how to write English, so they often couldn't communicate. To solve the problem of how to make sure clothes were returned to their proper owners, the laundry owners wrote Chinese descriptions of their patrons, instead of their names, on the brown paper laundry packages. As a way to

Ontario Archives, 10021917.

Chinese laundrymen earned between eight and eighteen dollars per month working and living in cramped space at the back of the laundry.

ensure that customers could get their laundry, tickets were given as receipts. George Heron, who wrote a memoir about growing up in Toronto, guessed what would happen if a customer lost his ticket: "I can imagine the trouble they would have had collecting their goods, trying to convince someone who spoke little or no English."[1]

These were the days of door-to-door service. Bread men and milkmen drove horse-drawn carts, parked in the street, and delivered their goods right to the door. Peddlers sold fruits and vegetables from a cart or the back of a truck. Even doctors made house calls. Naturally, laundry service included home delivery.

Edward Lamb.

Dennis Chow stands at the entrance of his Chow Keong Hand Laundry, one of the last Chinese hand laundries in Toronto.

Profile

Chow Keung arrived in Canada in 1921 at the age of fifteen, and worked at one of 374 Chinese laundries operating in Toronto at the time. He opened his own laundry in 1946 on Avenue Road, just north of Davenport. In 1952 he sponsored his son, Dennis, to join him in Toronto. Now aged seventy-nine, Dennis still works with his wife at the Chow Keung Hand Laundry.

There was little in the way of making the workday easier or more pleasant. One laundryman remembered those days, starting off at 6:00 a.m. to light a fire in the stove:

"We had to boil the water in a big pot and then pour it into the washing machine. It was very hard work." Afterwards, he washed the clothes and hung them up to dry. Then he'd press the clothes using a heavy iron that had been heated on a potbelly stove. He had to chop wood for the stove, keep a pile of coal, and keep the fires going throughout the day. This was his life, day after day.[2]

• • •

No Shortage of Ketchup

The second most popular Chinese businesses were restaurants and cafés. Some opened right in Chinatown and served Cantonese-style food to Chinese diners. However, those were the days when very few who weren't Chinese ventured into Chinatown. So, other Chinese restaurants were opened, located outside of Chinatown, where Western food such as roast beef, apple pie, and ice cream were served to cater to a non-Chinese clientele. Slowly, Chinese food, adapted for Canadian tastes, was added to the menus. The first Chinese restaurant in Toronto, Sing Tom, opened in 1901, where the present-day Bay department store is located at Queen and Yonge Streets.

Profile

"Chinese were also to be found running restaurants in certain parts of the city, offering cheap meals. This was a bonanza for the many unemployed men who crowded the city during the Depression years. On Queen Street near Sherbourne there were a couple of these restaurants, which offered full course meals for fifteen cents. [F]ull course … meant soup, a Salisbury steak or fish main course, with vegetables, a piece of pie and a drink of tea, coffee or milk. Not only that, each table had plates piled high with white and brown bread. And there was no shortage of ketchup, which the patrons liberally applied to their bread or added to their soup."[3]

~ George Heron

Toronto Archives, Fonds 200, Series 372, Sub-series 33, Item 171.

Some Chinese restaurants were located outside of Chinatown; there they served Western food, and later on, Chinese food. Others, like the one shown in Chinatown at 56 Elizabeth Street, catered to an exclusively Chinese clientele.

By 1921 the Chinese population in Toronto was 2,134, and there were 358 Chinese laundries, thirty-two restaurants, and nine other businesses, like grocery stores. Toronto's Chinatown was now the third largest in Canada, after Victoria and Vancouver.

• • •

A Dark Cloud

All the head taxes, as expensive as they were, did not stop the Chinese from coming. In fact the Chinese population in Canada doubled from seventeen thousand to thirty-seven thousand between 1901 and 1921. Although Toronto's Chinatown was becoming a bustling centre, a new law dropped a dark cloud over the Chinese community for the next twenty-four years.

On July 1, 1923, the Chinese Immigration Act, also known as the Chinese Exclusion Act, was passed by the Canadian government. Virtually all Chinese were now barred from entering Canada, the few exceptions being diplomats, merchants, and students. Also, any Chinese, whether they were born or living in Canada, had to report to the Canadian government to be registered. The penalty for non-compliance was a jail sentence or hefty fine.

Every year on July 1, when the rest of Canadians celebrated Dominion Day, now called Canada Day, the Chinese refused to join in any festivities. For them July 1 was "Humiliation Day," the day that the Chinese in Canada suffered the indignity of government racism at its worst.

In Chinatown the stores and restaurants were closed. There were no flags anywhere in sight. Children were not allowed to go to any playgrounds. No Chinese dared to participate in any Dominion Day celebrations,

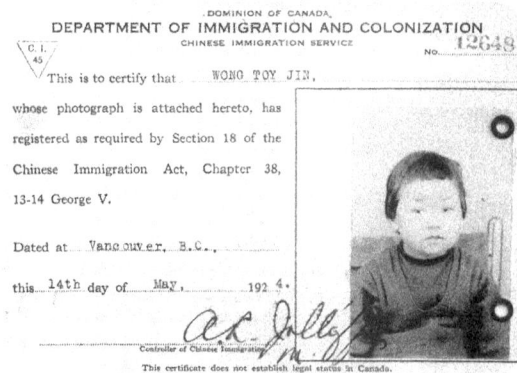

Jean Lumb Collection.

When the Chinese Exclusion Act was implemented in 1923, all Chinese, even Canadian-born children, had to be registered for an identification card. This is the one for Wong Toy Jin (Jean Lumb), who was four years old.

like parades. If they did they would have faced shame within their community, and their names would have been printed in the Chinese newspapers.

THREE

Living in Chinatown

In the 1920s Toronto was bigger and busier than ever. People had steady jobs and families and a place to live. There was plenty of food to go around. The economy was booming, and more and more immigrants were arriving. Until that time most of the people living in Toronto had a British background, but now thousands were arriving from other parts of Europe to live and work in the city. Immigrants from Poland and Ukraine worked in the stockyards and meat-packing plants in the Junction at Keele and Dundas Streets. Kensington Market attracted Jews from Russia and Eastern Europe. Blacks from the Caribbean lived around Front and Sherbourne Streets.

For the Chinese the story was quite different. The Chinese Exclusion Act of 1923 stopped the influx of Chinese immigrants. None were arriving, and most of the Chinese living in Toronto at the time were males. The explanation for the predominance of men is simple. With few exceptions, only men had left China to come to Canada. The early need for young, strong male workers to build the railway and the expensive head taxes had served as strong deterrents to female immigration. As well, tradition and social customs in China served to discourage women from leaving with their men. In the latter part of the nineteenth century and the early years of the twentieth century, Chinese women were a rarity in Toronto. In fact, the arrival of Lock Quong's wife in 1909 was deemed newsworthy enough for it to be noted on page one of the *Toronto Daily Star* on October 11 that year.

In all of the Chinese communities in Canada, men far outnumbered women, so much so that the communities came to be known as bachelor societies. Some of the men were actually single; however, 80 percent of the 29,033 Chinese men in Canada were in fact married, but their wives were in China.[1] In 1931 the male-female ratio was twelve Chinese men to one Chinese female. In Toronto only a handful of Chinese men had families: thirteen, in all.

George Heron recorded a sombre observation in his memoir: "Those who lived or ran a business in Chinatown were mainly middle-aged [or] elderly males, and they tended to stay in the area. There were virtually no Chinese women and I don't remember seeing any children of that race."[2]

Others, like Tom MacInnes, were less sympathetic than Heron: "The Chinese cannot rightly be said to be separated by any Canadian law from their wives and children in China. They are free to go back to their wives and children in China any time; and God speed them!"[3]

• • •

Short-Lived Happiness

For the Chinese men in Toronto, being forced to live without women and children resulted in a great deal of loneliness. Life without a family was unimaginable for them, so foreign to Chinese culture and tradition. Due to the Chinese Exclusion Act, there was no chance of bringing families to Canada. Many men returned to China rather than face a life apart from their families. Others remained to keep earning money to send home and to save enough for visits to their villages.

Cheng Ying-wai, who came to Canada in 1914, remembered this era: "The whole city of Toronto didn't have a dozen Chinese women in 1946…. We had no family to go home to [in Toronto]. I returned to China three times to see my family, but I couldn't bring them back with me."[4]

Anyone, like Cheng Ying-wai, who made visits home, was welcomed back to his village with much celebration and was treated like a celebrity. These were the men who sent money home so that their families could buy food to eat and pay their rent and taxes. These men were also the benefactors for their villages, helping them to build schools, roads, and hospitals.

The men told stories about life in Gold Mountain, often overinflating their successes, and brought news of others who had left their villages. Most importantly, they spent precious time with their wives and families. They knew that the longest they could stay was two years; otherwise, they would not be allowed back into Canada.

Along with the husbands returning to China to visit their wives and families, single men went, too, looking for a wife. Girls, as young as sixteen, were selected as suitable brides for arranged marriages to these men. Such marriages were sometimes made with the assistance of a matchmaker. Any girl who married someone from Gold Mountain was considered lucky. However, this happiness was short-lived, for inevitably her newly wedded husband would leave her and return alone to Canada. Future visits by husbands were rare or so infrequent that these women ended up living a lonely existence — like a widow, a Gold Mountain widow.

• • •

Sam Who?

Not only did Chinese immigrants to Canada have to leave their families behind, they frequently had to leave their names, or parts of them, behind, too. There are many differences between Chinese naming practices and Western ones; Canadian officials, not to mention the general population, did not understand and were not interested in trying to understand those differences. As a result most Chinese changed — or were forced to change — their names.

Chinese names consist of three parts: the surname and two given names. The surname appears first. One of the two given names is a generation name that is usually shared by others born in the same generation such as brothers and cousins. The other is a personal name.

Yip Kew Dock, Canada's first Chinese-Canadian lawyer, was called Mr. Yip since Yip was his surname. His generation name was Kew, shared by his eighteen brothers, like Yip Kew Shim. Dock was his personal name.

In Canada people often followed Western practice and changed the traditional Chinese name order by putting their given names before their surnames. This is what Yip Kew Dock did. He used the Westernized name order of Kew Dock Yip. He was called Dock by his friends.

A naming tradition common amongst the Chinese adds further complexity to their names. While people of British and European ancestry have one or two given names, such as James or Edward, a Chinese man has different ones throughout his life. These can include a baby name, a school name, and a married name.

All of this can be very confusing to a non-Chinese person. Records of Chinese coming into Canada and living in the city were documented by the government, but because the early record-keepers did not speak or write Chinese, they simply recorded the Chinese names as closely as possible based on what they heard. That is why the early records of the Chinese are so incomplete and often misleading. The English-speaking officials who recorded the names of the immigrants were not able to write the Chinese names consistently in English from year to year.

To make things even more confusing, it's common when Chinese talk about someone for them to start his or her name with the word *ah*. The use of "ah" at the beginning of a name in Chinese is like the use of "ie" or "y" at the end of someone's name in English — John becomes Johnny or Johnnie. "Ah" is not part of anyone's name in Chinese, but it often ended up in official records, and so one finds Ah Chong instead of Chong.

Something else that added to confusion in government records was the practice of government officials giving English names to early Chinese immigrants. For example when the Chinese first began to arrive in Toronto the name *Sam* was very common. Sam Ching was the first Chinese man with that name to be listed in Toronto's records; he appears in documents from 1878. Later other *Sams* had businesses and laundries, such as Sam Lee on Jarvis Street, Sam Sing on Queen Street West, and Sam Wing on Adelaide Street. These individuals were known as Sam in English, but their Chinese given names would have been used by their friends and relatives.

As time passed more and more Chinese, especially those born in Canada, had Chinese and English names. One man remembered being upset as a child for having to keep his Chinese name. The solution? At home and in Chinatown he was called Man-fei. At school he was known as Murphy, an English name that sounded like his Chinese name.[5]

Depending on when a person's name was recorded, which English-speaking person recorded it, and at what time in the person's life it was recorded, a Chinese person could appear in various government records under totally different names. That is why, to this day, it remains a challenge to research and trace family histories from these early years.

• • •

Family and County Associations

In China there are about one thousand surnames. The most prevalent among the early Chinese immigrants in Canada were Lee, Lem, Wong, and Chan. Although people

Wong Family Association.

In 2011 the Wongs were the first Chinese in Canada to have a coat of arms. The family crest depicts a panda bear, a polar bear, and a phoenix.

with the same surname are not necessarily blood relatives, they likely share the same ancestor in the distant past. It is not unusual for most of the people from a village to have the same surname.

In Canada Chinese immigrants with the same surname formed family associations. Among the early family associations were the Li She Kong So (Lee Association) and Lem Si Ho Tong (Lem Society); these can still be found in Chinatown. Another long-standing association is Lung Kong Kung So, whose membership is made up of people with four surnames: Liu (Lew, Low), Guan (Kwan, Quan, Quon), Zhang (Cheung, Chong), and Zhao (Chu, Chew).

The Wong Wun Sun King So (Wong Association) is another early family association that is still active today. Wong is the seventh most popular surname in China, and there are thirty-nine million Wongs around the world.[6] The first Wong in Canada was recorded in 1858 and the first Chinese baby born in Canada was a Wong — Won Alexander Cumyow.

Chinese Canadians also formed other associations, establishing them for people from the same counties or geographic districts, for example. Kwong Hoi Hui Kuan had members who were from the district of Kwong Hoi. The Chinese kept a strong connection to their home village and considered themselves part of it, no matter how great the distance they were from home.

Membership in these associations had its benefits because they supported the Chinese in their efforts to establish a life in Toronto. As well as providing a place to socialize, these organizations provided help for immigration, taxes, illness, interpreting, letter-writing, employment, emergencies, and money remittances to families in China. They found places for homeless men, and solved problems among their members or with non-Chinese people. There is a Chinese saying: "Don't wash your dirty laundry in public." Rarely would any Chinese go outside of their associations for help of any sort.

Another responsibility of the associations was looking after their deceased members. The Chinese believed that it was important to be buried in their ancestral home; otherwise, they'd become wandering ghosts in a foreign country. By Chinese custom bodies were interred in a simple burial. After seven years the bodies were dug up from the cemetery, like the Mount Pleasant Cemetery in Toronto. The bones were then cleaned and packed in wooden crates to send to China. Once there the bones were buried in family cemeteries alongside the ancestors of the deceased. The last shipment of bones was shipped in 1936.[7]

Lastly, an important function of the associations was the banking system. Members who wanted to buy a business or purchase supplies, furniture, and equipment had to rely on their associations for loans. The Chinese could not borrow money from Canadian banks until the 1960s.

The Wong Association of Ontario is located in Chinatown West.

Jens Romzeberger.

• • •

What does it look like inside an association building? Not much has changed since those early years. Typically, there are pictures of members and leaders, banners, paintings, and lists of donors on the walls. In a key spot there is usually a shrine that has a portrait of an ancestor or legendary forefather and a table with burning incense, flowers, and plates of food, such as cakes and fruits. Poems or historical messages that are beautifully written in large calligraphy usually frame both sides of the portrait.

What is often referred to as ancestor worship is not as religious as it sounds. Once living persons, these ancestors are respected and honoured by their descendants. As an example, Guan Gong (166–219), is one of the most famous generals of Chinese history. Easily recognizable by his bright red face and long black beard, he represents honour, loyalty, integrity, justice, courage, and strength. On special days such as holidays or festivals, the members gather in front of the shrine and bow three times to the portrait of the ancestor as a gesture of respect.

• • •

Political Associations

For people in Toronto interested in what was happening in China, political associations were created. So much was changing in China, and these associations served to provide information, sponsor discussions, and, on occasion, coordinate responses.

The collapse of the Qing dynasty was a spur for the creation of some of these.

As the Chinese began arriving in Toronto, the Qing dynasty, which had been established in 1644, was losing its grip on the country. China faced peasant uprisings and civil wars because of the inability of the Qing government to limit foreign trade and incursions by foreign military forces.

At the core of the problem was the trade in tea. Every year China exported millions of kilograms of tea leaves to Britain to satisfy the demand of British citizens for tea. In order to create a source of revenue for itself to offset the import of tea, Britain flooded China with opium. Although the Chinese had long used opium for medicinal purposes, the British sold it for use as a recreational drug. Opium was so addictive that it turned millions of Chinese into drug addicts. The Qing government tried to stop the import of opium; however, British merchants refused to accept the government's ban. When the government compelled them to, Britain responded with force. So began the first of the two Opium Wars. It lasted from 1839 to 1842. Another followed in 1856, lasting to 1860. China lost both wars against Britain. As a result of its loss, China was compelled to hand over Hong Kong to Britain; it was also forced to accept the occupation of the rest of China by Britain and other European countries.

The Chinese became second-class citizens in their own country. The port city of Shanghai, for example, was divided into French, American, English, and Japanese concessions, or sectors, each with its own prisons, police, schools, and hospitals, which were governed by the laws of each respective country. The Chinese were not allowed into these concessions and Chinese laws and taxes didn't apply there.

On top of those insults, China was required to pay enormous fines as a penalty for the cost of the war — fines that emptied its treasury and necessitated increased taxation of the Chinese. All of this brought much economic hardship, which led to a big increase in banditry and looting. Added to these woes were natural disasters — floods, earthquakes, and droughts — that caused food shortages and starvation.

A radical change was needed to save China from its spiral downwards. Some Chinese believed that the Qing government merely needed to institute political reform and modernization to deal with the issues. Others believed that the only way to save China was to overthrow the Qing dynasty, oust the foreign occupiers, and re-establish Chinese rule. Such differences

of political opinion were at the root of the uprisings and civil wars in China. The Boxer Rebellion (1898–1900), as an example, tried to overthrow the Manchu government and rid China of all of the foreigners from countries such as Britain, Germany, France, and Russia.

In Canada two opposing political organizations were established. On one side was the Chinese Empire Reform Association, which supported the Manchu government and believed its reform would save China. On the other side, the Chinese Freemasons Association held the position that nothing short of a complete political change was needed in China.

One important political leader who visited Canada during this period was Dr. Sun Yat-sen. He was a man who believed that the Manchu government in China should end and a new government be established. Because of his revolutionary ideas, he was banished from China. As an exile he travelled extensively, touring North America and other parts of the world to promote an overthrow of the government in China. His rousing and passionate speeches touched the hearts of the overseas Chinese, who donated generous amounts of money for his cause.

A bronze statue of Sun Yat-sen, remembered as the father of modern China, is prominently located in Riverdale Park, close to Chinatown East.

Sam Eng remembered meeting him during one of his visits to Toronto: "He came to raise money to buy munitions and guns and take them back to the revolution. The only trouble is he didn't stay long enough. He [came] on Wednesday, [left] on Saturday. We talked but not long enough to learn everything he learned."[8]

In 1911 the Manchus were overthrown. After 267 years their Qing dynasty came to an end, and the Republic of China was founded. Chinese men were finally allowed to cut off their queues, the hairstyle that had been forced on them by the Manchus.

The Guomindang, the Chinese Nationalist Party, was established in the new China, a political party that came to be known in Toronto as the Chinese Nationalist League. Its weekly newspaper, *Shing Wah*, printed on Hagerman Street, was one of the largest Chinese newspapers in the Dominion of Canada.

• • •

Three Ways Flow Into One

Various associations helped the Chinese in Canada keep in touch with their communities; another important link for them was their cultural and religious traditions. Like all immigrants the Chinese brought their beliefs and customs with them when they came to Canada, and practising these helped them to feel more at home in a new and hostile country.

The teachings of Confucius formed an important part of those beliefs. Confucius (Kong Fuzi) was the most influential teacher and philosopher in China. He lived from 551 to 479 BCE, a time when the government was very disorganized. He made many suggestions to improve its relationship with the people. Confucius taught that if everyone showed respect, kindness, and obedience, then everything would run smoothly. According to his teachings, people should respect the emperor, the son, his father, the wife her husband, and so on. Confucius also strongly emphasized the importance of education and family life, which he considered the foundation of society and government. According to him every man was linked by his surname to his parents, grandparents, and ancestors, from generation to generation.

Another man who greatly influenced Chinese life was Laozi. He believed that people should live in harmony with the universe, and maintain a simple life, one without the distractions of ambition, wealth, and power. Life should be in tune with the natural rhythms of day and night, and other repeating cycles, such as the four seasons of spring, summer, fall, and winter. Laozi believed that a balance of the world's energy forces, yin and yang, was needed for harmony. Cold balanced hot, feminine balanced masculine, and so on. Laozi's philosophy later became the foundation for the religion of Daoism.

A statue of Confucius was unveiled at the Chinese Cultural Centre of Greater Toronto in 1999 on the occasion of his 550th birthday.

Another important figure for many Chinese was Buddha. He was an Indian nobleman who lived during the sixth and fifth centuries BCE. He gave up his riches to learn how to overcome suffering and to reach an enlightened state called *nirvana* through meditation and acts of kindness. Unlike Confucianism and Daoism, which were created in China, Buddhism was brought to China from India, arriving over two thousand years ago. It evolved in China, keeping the main features of Indian Buddhism but changing over time. Eventually, Chinese Buddhism had many distinct features.

Today some Chinese are Buddhists or Daoists who go to temples. Others blend practices and beliefs in their day to day lives. They follow the Confucian philosophy of respect and honour for their families, enjoy the beauty of nature for Daoist peace of mind, and live their lives upholding the moral principles of Buddhism. According to one ancient Chinese saying, "The three ways flow into one."

The practice of making offerings to gods, goddesses, and ancestors extends beyond temples into many homes and businesses. Stores

The Cham Shan Temple is one of North America's largest Buddhist temples. In former times Chinese temples were often called joss houses by non-Chinese people because of the practice of burning joss sticks or incense.

sell porcelain statues and posters of gods, and packages of incense and paper money to burn on special occasions such as birthdays and festivals. At the entrance or interior of some stores, shops, and restaurants in Chinatown, there are altar boxes with a statue of a Chinese god, like the god of wealth, along with incense and fruit.

Jens Ronneberger.

To bring good luck, many Chinese keep shrines in their homes and stores. This one is at the entrance of a bakery in Chinatown West.

• • •

Churches

When the Chinese began settling in Toronto, churches and missionary workers reached out to the newcomers. During the decades of anti-Chinese discrimination, churches were among the few non-Chinese groups that helped the Chinese, and they provided an important service. As early as 1894, Toronto churches were offering English classes to the Chinese so that they could read the Bible and adopt Christian life.

The Chinese wanted to learn English to be more accepted into Canadian society, but they found the foreign language very difficult. The words were read from left to right instead of from top to bottom as in Chinese writing, and English words were composed of letters from an alphabet so different from the Chinese words or characters that were formed by a combination of brush strokes. The sounds of English words were also very different. Despite these challenges the Chinese took full advantage of the English classes provided by the churches. By 1910 almost half of the one thousand Chinese in Toronto were studying English.

Another important contribution of the churches was the help they gave the Chinese to get an education beyond their English classes. Chinese women, from British Columbia in particular, were financially sponsored to move to other provinces — or even to China — to study. The education provided to them helped them to find jobs.

It wasn't always easy for the early Chinese to get education, though. For example, British Columbia didn't allow the Chinese to study medicine, pharmacy, and other professions; on the other hand, however, Ontario had no such restriction. As a result women from British Columbia, like Victoria Cheung, moved to Toronto to enrol at the School of Medicine of the University of Toronto. In 1923 she was the first Chinese student there; she went on to become the first woman to intern at the Toronto General Hospital, and the first female Chinese-Canadian doctor. Her church in Vancouver made all of these breakthroughs possible. In the same year, Agnes Chan was another Chinese-Canadian woman who came to Toronto from British Columbia. Chan studied and graduated from the Women's College Hospital School of Nursing as its first Chinese nurse.

The first Chinese church in Toronto opened in 1910 as the Toronto Chinese Young Men's Christian Institute. Other early ones include the Chinese Presbyterian Church and the Chinese United Church. Today there are many Chinese churches in Chinatown, as well as others around the Greater Toronto Area. With the influx of Chinese immigrants, church membership has increased, and Sunday services are offered in many Chinese churches in Cantonese, Mandarin, and/or English. In Markham, for example, two Catholic churches are baptizing more than six hundred Chinese people a year.[9] Churchgoers can find not only religion but also social support, friendship, and settlement services.

• • •

Crazy for Opera

While religion continues to play an important role in the lives of many Chinese, the arts and culture are very important, too. The same was true in the past. After World War One, music and opera were important pastimes and sources of entertainment in Toronto's Chinatown. The Chinese were crazy for opera, an art form loved for over eight hundred years. Although there are different styles of opera, the early immigrants particularly enjoyed Cantonese opera, because it was popular in their homeland. At the opera one could forget, for a while, about the bad times and enjoy the exciting stories that were brought alive on stage. While the orchestra played music with traditional Chinese instruments, warriors, villains, generals, gods, and demons played out tales of romance and history with colourful costumes, painted faces, and dazzling movements.

The best known style today is Beijing opera. It is very traditional, and opera lovers understand the meaning of all the costumes, the faces, and the movements of the actors as they sing and fill the stage with their acrobatic moves and martial arts. Yellow dragon gowns are for emperors. Heroes' faces are painted in red, black, and purple; villains in white and yellow; warriors in blue and green; and ghosts in gold and silver. If the actor holds a long stick with tassels, he is riding a horse. If his character is angry, he steps back and flings his long sleeves out in front.

Perfecting operatic roles takes a lifetime of learning. In the past young boys from poor families were sold to an opera school as young as the age of eight. Students practised from morning to night under a master who whipped or beat the boys for making even the slightest

Starlight Chinese Opera.

The Starlight Chinese Opera, featuring here Eliza Kam (left) and Alice Chan (right), performs and teaches opera.

mistakes. Holding a handstand for forty minutes or staying in a crouched position for an hour were not uncommon in the daily drills. Today the schools are much less severe and the education is more well-rounded.

Northern Legs Southern Fists.

Actor and martial artist Jackie Chan (centre), pictured in Toronto with Sifu Ian Chow (left), started training at the school of the Peking Opera when he was seven years old.

Chinese operas lasted for hours, so audience members could get up from their seats and move around during the performance. This was perfect for children, because they didn't have to sit for hours at a time. If they got bored, they could run around the theatre and play with their friends.

The first Chinese opera houses opened in Toronto in the 1930s. Gordon Chong, a fourth-generation Chinese Canadian who was a Toronto city councillor, has fond memories of the opera: "I remember living on Queen Street, between University and York, on the second floor above some stores. We used to go to Chinese theatre on Sundays at the Casino Theatre. There used to be Chinese opera and we'd play around backstage."[10]

Valerie Mah, Chinatown historian and Toronto's first Chinese-Canadian school principal, recalled her family coming to Toronto from her hometown in Brockville: "We'd catch the Chinese opera, seeing people pushing chairs around that were pretend lions.... We'd visit my uncle, Henry Lore, at 109 Dundas Street. Then we'd stay at the Ford Hotel, which was on the corner of Bay and Dundas, where the Atrium is now."[11]

• • •

Chinese Medicine

The entertainment offered to the Chinese by the opera provided only a short break. Mostly, their lives were filled with hard work and the struggle to get by. In such circumstances they couldn't afford to become ill — and if they did, they needed a way to get better quickly. Most of the early Chinese immigrants, like the gold prospectors and railway workers, for example, relied on traditional Chinese medicine if they got sick or injured. They used Chinese herbs and remedies partly because they believed these would help them and partly because they couldn't get treatment from Western doctors.

All kinds of herbs, leaves, flowers, powders, and ginseng roots have been used in Chinese medicine for over two thousand years to treat ailments from headaches to ulcers. As well as using such common plant material, Chinese medicines sometimes use dried animals parts, too, such as tiger testicles, seal penises, beef tongues, and deer antlers for treating health problems. Many animals are now endangered due to their use in Chinese medicine. In order to save these animals, laws have been introduced in countries around the world. Efforts are also being made to encourage alternatives that are non-endangered and plant-based.

Typically, a Chinese doctor will examine a patient's tongue and eyes, and check the pulse at the wrist. He will then make a diagnosis and create a prescription. Based on the prescription, the herbalist will carefully weigh dried herbs, pieces of bark and twigs, and other items. Some things are ground up by mortar and pestle before they are wrapped in paper. At home this mixture of five to twenty ingredients is boiled, strained, and swallowed like tea. The awful taste and offensive smell are enough to make anyone want to run away as far as possible. But it's not supposed to taste good, it's supposed to do good.

Acupuncture is another form of Chinese medicine; it involves the painless insertion of small, thin needles at certain points of the body to help in a natural healing process. This procedure is widely used today, even by athletes at the Olympic Games.

Chinese-Canadian patients began to seek non-Chinese medicine as well, and from early on a handful of Western-trained Chinese doctors opened their medical offices in Chinatown. Their practices were mostly restricted to their fellow Chinese-Canadians. One such doctor was Philip Chu, who graduated as a doctor from the University of Toronto in 1925. He had an office on Hagerman Street. One day there was an accident on Elizabeth and Dundas streets: a man was seriously injured in a collision with a streetcar. Dr. Chu was quickly summoned from his nearby office to the accident scene. As he opened his medical bag, the wife of the injured man yelled out, "I don't want no Chink touching my husband."[12]

Things changed, though, and Chinese-Canadian doctors eventually became more and more part of the wider medical establishment in Toronto. Dr. Henry Lore, for example, graduated from medical school at the University of Toronto in 1939 and opened his office at 109 Dundas Street. Not only was he a staff physician at the Toronto General Hospital, he was an important leader in the Chinese community and president of the Chinese Freemasons Association.

• • •

The Dirty Thirties

The 1920s was a decade of setbacks and advances for the Chinese in Toronto. The Chinese Exclusion Act of 1923 had been a terrible blow, and its effect lasted for a long time. However, there were gains, too, with many Chinese becoming more established financially and gaining access to more education. There were still many problems, but things were getting better. Everything changed, though, at the end of the decade.

October 29, 1929, is the day remembered as Black Tuesday. The stock market crashed. Soon after businesses went bankrupt, banks shuttered their doors, stores closed down, factories laid off thousands of workers. This infamous day started the "Dirty Thirties" or "Hungry Thirties," a decade few Canadians were prepared for or expected. No one could afford to buy things, and that put even more people out of work. Soon, nearly 30 percent of Canadians were unemployed.

Within a few years, one in four Torontonians was on relief, relying on the city for food and vouchers for rent and fuel. Hungry people formed long, winding lineups at soup kitchens, churches, wherever there was food to be had. Children dragged wagons along the streets and railway tracks looking for stray lumps of coal to heat their homes.

People had to repair, reuse, make do, and not throw anything away. Socks were mended and patches were sewn over holes in clothes. Children wore hand-me-down clothing from their older brothers and sisters. Overcoats were relined with old blankets. Shoes were stuffed with cardboard when the soles wore through.

The Canadian government worried that Chinese Canadians would overwhelm the country's already-stretched resources. To avoid the cost of providing them any support, one-way tickets to China were offered to the Chinese. Many accepted and left Canada without ever returning. Those who stayed turned to their associations for financial help because the Chinese didn't like to take their troubles outside of their own community.

Even though unemployment among the Chinese in Canada was higher than average, only fifty Chinese out of two thousand applied for the government's help when it was offered in Toronto. The city was not a happy place for ten long and hard years of the Great Depression.

Profile

Sam Eng worked from the day of his arrival in Canada in 1905 as a thirteen-year-old until his retirement at age seventy-four. He was the only one of five children who left China with his father to make money for the whole family. Because his father couldn't afford to send him to school, Eng worked as a bell hop at a hotel from 3 p.m. to midnight. He was proud to say that he never collected unemployment insurance or government assistance of any kind.[13]

FOUR

A Child's Life

In early Toronto, growing up was nothing like it is today. There were no social services, so the impact of world events and local circumstances were felt with great force by the working-class families and their children — wherever they or their parents came from. The children of wealthy and middle-class families could afford to have a childhood, but it was very different for everyone else. Instead of being at school during the day and playing afterwards, the children of the working class did whatever they could to earn a few pennies to help with their family's food and rent expenses. School was not compulsory until 1871. They worked in factories for ten or twelve hours a day, or sewed shirts and overcoats at home. They stood on street corners selling newspapers or shining shoes. Girls as young as eight years of age were left at home to look after their younger brothers and sisters while both their parents worked. Some children resorted to begging and shoplifting to make ends meet.

Profile

Ernest C. Mark was twelve years old when he came to Toronto in 1908. After school he worked at his father's store in Chinatown. Because he could speak English, he got a good job working for the Canadian Pacific Railway and, became the unofficial mayor of Toronto's Chinatown for the English-speaking community. He was also a prominent elder at the Chinese Presbyterian Church and publisher of the *Shing Wah* newspaper.

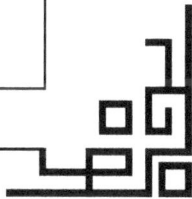

Being a child of immigrants had its challenges, as is the case today. Immigrant parents cling to their homeland values, long for the familiarity of their life in their home country, and ache in loneliness for the loved ones left behind. They have to adapt to a foreign culture and country while struggling to earn a living. For the early Chinese immigrants in Toronto, the comforts found in Chinatown, which gave them a sense of belonging, could not overcome their feelings of isolation and culture shock.

The children of immigrants, on the other hand, yearn to become as Canadianized as possible. Whether born in Toronto or in China, the children adapt more easily to the differences in their cultural background and the larger community.

Going to school is one way to learn about the Canadian way of life. By 1900 children in Toronto had to go to school up to the age of twelve. By 1921 children were required to attend school until the age of sixteen. Children who lived in and near Chinatown attended York Public School, Odgen School, Orde Street School, or Hester How School — the latter of these is now part of the site of the Hospital for Sick Children. Speaking English all day at

Profile

In 1922, at the age of five, James Pon came to Canada with his mother. The head tax was five hundred dollars for each of them, and it took seventeen years for his father to repay the one thousand dollars he had borrowed to bring them over. Although the law required attendance at school, Pon had to work instead. "In those days there was a recession in Canada. As a youngster I had to go out and work.... I had to earn my own living at twelve years old. Imagine that?"[1] He served tables, cleaned floors, and washed dishes. Through hard work, he earned enough to go to university. Eventually, Pon graduated and found work as an engineer for de Havilland, the company that built the Mosquito bomber used in World War Two. He is currently president of the Foundation to Commemorate the Chinese Railroad Workers in Canada.

Mavis Lew Collection.

This Grade 1 and 2 class at Hester How School had twelve Chinese-Canadian students in 1947.

school naturally led to a desire to speak it at home and at other times, especially with their brothers and sisters. This upset their parents, who strongly valued the preservation of the Chinese language and who upheld an unpopular expectation for their children to learn Chinese.

• • •

The Bottom Line

Learning to speak and write Chinese was not very popular amongst Chinese children. Of course, children were expected to learn English, because this was really important for living in Toronto. More often than not, their parents relied on them in any dealings with non-Chinese people. The bottom line, however, was that everyone had to also speak Chinese.

William C. Wong, who became a prominent leader of the Chinese Community Centre and president of the Shing Wah newspaper, teaches a class at Chinese school.

One Canadian-born Chinese woman, who grew up in Cabbagetown, didn't have any Chinese friends. "I remember when we'd go down to Chinatown on Sundays with my dad, people would laugh at us because we couldn't speak Chinese. The assumption was that if you looked Chinese, you should be able to speak Chinese.... Chinese people would actually point and laugh at us!"[2]

In the early years, children were taught Chinese by untrained teachers, taking their lessons at the back of their family laundries, restaurants, or stores. Eventually, Chinese schools, the first opening in 1914, were set up hockey or other games, children sat through two more hours of lessons learning how to read and write Chinese. This schooling was valued as very important by their families.

Not only was education important, so were manners. Parents expected their children to make a good impression wherever they were. The parents believed that poor behaviour disgraced not only a child's family but also all the Chinese living in Toronto. Getting into trouble at school, in the playground, anywhere, was not taken lightly. The Chinese community was so small at the time, and word about bad behaviour would certainly have travelled back to their parents.

• • •

In The Days Before Video Games

When the children weren't in school they hung around the neighbourhood. The streets were a huge playground, and Chestnut Street was a favourite spot to play, because the traffic was not too busy. Hillock's Lumberyard, which was located on Chestnut Street, was closed on the weekends and so was a particularly popular place to hang out. The boys played marbles while the girls took turns at street games such as hopscotch and skipping

Maris Lew Collection.

Nine-year-old Gene poses in front of his dad's barber shop at 117 Elizabeth Street in Chinatown in 1954. Although most customers were Chinese, non-Chinese patrons were never turned away and a sign in the window proclaimed NO DISCRIMINATION.

for children to learn in formal classroom settings. Every day after regular school they had to go to Chinese school. Instead of playing rope. The nearby Land Registry building was also popular because the large columns and grand outdoor staircase made the games of tag and hide-and-seek so much more fun

On Saturdays, a bunch of boys would meet at the Central YMCA at 40 College Street to work out in the gym or play sports such as softball or basketball. They not only enjoyed playing these sports, they became very good at them — so much so that in 1935 the Toronto Chinese Basketball Team won the Ontario Championships. This was such a proud accomplishment in the Chinese community that a celebratory dinner was held at the Royal York Hotel.

On Sundays the children attended Sunday school at the church, and if anyone lived far away, transportation was arranged. The church also provided a place where the boys liked to play badminton. They had to fix up old birdies again and again because they couldn't afford to buy new ones.

John Boyd/Library and Archives Canada/PA-083871.

While the girls joined CGIT (Canadian Girls in Training) or Brownies at the church, the boys signed up for Boy Scouts. A troop of Chinese Boy Scouts is pictured here eating lemons in High Park in 1919.

Mavis Lew Collection.

A class of Sunday school children at the Bay Street Church is pictured with Reverend William D. Noyes, who helped to fight anti-Chinese laws.

On a hot summer day, when it was too hot to stay indoors at home, popular destinations included movie theatres and the downtown department stores such as Eaton's and Simpson's. No one had air conditioning in their homes back then, and the cool theatres and stores offered relief — for a while, at least. The boys could go swimming at the YMCA. It was alright to swim in the buff then because women and girls weren't allowed anywhere at the Y. Sometimes relief was found from cooling chunks of ice that had fallen off the ice man's cart. Families relied on ice boxes that had to be filled with large blocks of ice, delivered once or twice a week by the ice man. Refrigerators didn't start appearing in homes until the 1930s.

During the winter months, playing in the snow was free and fun, but there was nothing better than lining the sidewalk to watch the Eaton's Santa Claus parade. This annual event started up in 1905 with only a few wagons pulled by horses, but later expanded with live reindeer, marching bands, and colourful floats. The end point was the Eaton's store, where Santa settled into his chair to listen to all the children with their toy lists. Another favourite was the Orange Parade, held every year on July 12 to celebrate the victory of the Protestant forces over the Catholic forces at the Battle of the Boyne in 1690. Thousands of marchers, walking to the music of many bands, made their way from Queen's Park to the Canadian National Exhibition. Leading the parade on a white, majestic horse was someone dressed up as William, Prince of Orange.

On other days of the year, children were content if they had a five-cent piece in their pockets for other sources of amusement. To earn it they would have run an errand for a neighbour or found things to sell such as pop, milk, and wine bottles, which were good for one- to five-cent refunds. Five cents paid for a hamburger, a hot dog, an order of French fries, or a double-scoop ice cream cone.

Their coins could also be used to pay for entertainment. Bowling was a popular pastime, and there was a handy bowling alley nearby on Terauley (later renamed Bay) Street; another one opened later on Elm Street. Even better than bowling was seeing two full-length movies and a cartoon at a Saturday matinee.

At home, reading provided most of the entertainment. Books could be borrowed from the public library. These were the days before computers, the Internet, video games, cell phones, and, for a long time, television. When all else failed, everyone crowded around the radio. In 1920 Canada broadcast its first radio programs. By 1930 most were American shows such as *The Shadow* and *The Shadow of Fu Manchu*.

While the parents expected their children to help out at their family businesses, get good grades at school, and strictly observe Chinese traditions, they also wanted their children to be happy. And life was happy for them, for the most part, living in Canada. However, there were years, too, when events outside of the country threatened the happiness of those living in Canada. These were the years when the worst of times unfolded.

FIVE

The War Years

World conflicts across the Atlantic Ocean and the Pacific Ocean were to involve virtually all Canadians one way or another, whether they remained at home or went overseas. Preceding and following the hard years of the Great Depression in the 1930s were two devastating world wars. Few Canadians anticipated the sacrifices that were to be demanded of Canada by these wars. Even fewer expected how their lives would be affected by the Sino-Japanese War in China.

• • •

World War One, 1914–1918

World War One, also known as "the Great War," broke out in 1914. The assassination of the heir to the Austro-Hungarian empire by a Serbian ignited the war flame. Austria-Hungary invaded Serbia, bringing Germany in as its ally.

Serbia had allied itself with Russia, France, and Britain, and they came to its defence. As a member of the British Empire, Canada was at war, too. In Toronto young men lined up at the Armouries building to join the army, the navy, or the Royal Flying Corps. Seventy thousand men, one seventh of the city's population, enlisted and received a rousing send-off as they boarded trains at Union Station.

Many Chinese in British Columbia tried to enlist in the Canadian army, but they were refused by recruiters on the grounds that this was a "white man's war." Undeterred, they travelled to other provinces, like Ontario, where they were allowed to sign up. One hope was that their war contribution would show their loyalty to Canada and convince the Canadian government to give them the right to vote. About three hundred Chinese volunteered for service in the Great War.

• • •

No Man's Land

The battlefields in Europe contained an elaborate network of trenches, tunnels, and underground shelters that stretched from the English Channel to Switzerland. Dug deep into the earth, these installations were easy to defend but dangerous to attack. Coils of barbed wire were spread in front of them, making it even harder for an enemy to attack. Between the trenches of the German troops and those of the Allied forces was a wasteland that came to be known as "No Man's Land."

At the best of times, life in the trenches was miserable. Rain, snow, mud, lice, and huge rats added more misery to the horrors caused by the enemy barrage of heavy artillery, snipers, and poison gas. Only occasionally would soldiers be fortunate enough to have a bath and clean underwear. Trench foot afflicted thousands with a disease caused by feet being wet and cold. Hunger was a constant preoccupation, despite the rations of food and the care packages from home.

How did these trenches and tunnels get built? At the beginning of the war, the soldiers built them, but as casualties increased there were not enough troops to do everything needed. So, China, at the request of Britain, provided two hundred thousand men as labourers to help extend and maintain the tunnels and trenches, and to do other necessary work. Known as the Chinese Labour Corps, they were recruited in 1916 to work on war projects for pay that was about four times what could have been earned in China. The British government officially referred to them as "coolies," and provided each recruit with a summer uniform, a winter uniform, and a fur-lined cap.

Canada helped the British government by transporting eighty thousand of these labourers from China to France. They crossed the Pacific Ocean by ship, and upon their arrival in British Columbia, their journey continued by train across Canada to the Maritime provinces. From seaports such as Halifax, Nova Scotia, and St. John's, Newfoundland, the men were transported by ship to their final destination in France, the trip taking three months from start to finish.

Once there the Chinese labourers were given a variety of tasks: loading and unloading supplies from ships and trains, filling sandbags, building roads and railways, and

C.P. Meredith/Library and Archives Canada/C-068863.

In 1917 several thousand workers from China, part of the Chinese Labour Corps, spent time in Petawawa, Ontario, before continuing their journey across Canada to France.

digging trenches. At the end of the war, they cleared the battlefields of corpses, ammunition, bombs, and grenades. Afterwards, all of the men were sent back to China, retracing the three-month route home. They were locked in the train cars, each guarded by four Canadian soldiers so that none of the Chinese "coolies" could escape.

At the time Canadians didn't know about these Chinese workers because Prime Minister Robert Borden ordered the strictest secrecy. A letter sent to the media by an immigration official in Ottawa stated the government's position: "The transport through Canada of a very large number of Chinese coolies [sic] will doubtless cause considerable comment and as it is desired that the movement shall occur without any publicity."[1]

> **Did You Know?**
>
> The word *coolie* is an outdated term that referred to labourers from China, India, and other countries in Asia who generally worked abroad. In Chinese, *kuli* means "bitter strength," although the exact origin of the English term is unknown.

• • •

A War To End All Wars

At the outset of the war, the United States was neutral. It remained so until 1917, when German U-boats sank seven American merchant ships bound for Europe. This act of aggression left Americans with no choice but to declare war on Germany. With the addition of tens of thousands of American troops, the Great War was soon over, ending on November 11, 1918. American President Woodrow Wilson declared it "a war to end all wars."

More than six hundred thousand men and a handful of women served in Canada's military forces — sixty-six thousand did not

return home, another 170,000 were wounded.[2] When the survivors arrived back in Canada, they wanted jobs, houses, and cars. For the Chinese-Canadian war veterans, they wanted the right to vote. In 1920 they were granted the vote; however, they didn't get to exercise that right because the Dominion Elections Act was introduced later in the same year. That act reinforced the law that stated that no Chinese were entitled to vote. Although this legislation was a huge disappointment to the Chinese in Canada, more unsettling news came from their homeland.

• • •

Civil War and the Sino-Japanese War

After the Manchu government was overthrown by the Chinese people in 1911, China was torn apart by more war and political unrest. The new government was weak, and many groups struggled to seize power. These included the Chinese Communist Party established by Mao Zedong (Mao Tse-tung), the Chinese Nationalist Party (Guomindang) under Chiang Kai-shek, and the warlords, military leaders who ruled various parts of China from 1916 to 1928. China was a divided country. In the

William and Elizabeth Wong Family Collection.

During the war parades with elaborate floats proceeded through Chinatown. Following the floats, a group of people carried a large flag to collect donations for the war effort in China.

1920s the Nationalist Party united temporarily with Communist supporters to fight the warlords and regain control of China. When the warlords were defeated, Chiang Kai-shek focused his military attention on eliminating Communism. However, this attempt was cut short because Japan, the greatest enemy of the Chinese people, attacked at this time.

The First Sino-Japanese War was fought between China and Japan from 1894 to 1895 over the control of Korea. China lost that war and handed over Taiwan to Japan. China subsequently engaged in minor skirmishes with

Japan; by 1937, these escalated into full-blown war, the Second Sino-Japanese War. Again, Mao Zedong and Chiang Kai-shek joined forces — this time to fight the Japanese. Even with the alliance of the Nationalists and the Communists, however, the Chinese couldn't defend their country. Most of China's largest cities, such as Beijing, Shanghai, and Nanjing, fell to the Japanese aggressors, and by 1940 Japan occupied most of China's other major cities.

The unstable conditions in China brought great anxiety to the Chinese in Canada. Even before the war, they could barely endure the heavy weight of the Chinese Exclusion Act that kept them apart from their families. With their homeland now occupied by the Japanese, being unable to learn of the whereabouts and safety of their loved ones was infinitely worse. Without much convincing, the Chinese across Canada rallied to the call for financial help for those in their homeland.

The Chinese in Toronto raised money to send to China to help in its fight against the Japanese. Clothes were collected to send to the soldiers. Medical supplies, even ambulances and airplanes, were purchased. Funds were raised for the war orphans. Women organized church bazaars where home-baked dishes and handmade clothing were sold. Ticket sales from Chinese opera and music performances raised money. Little did the Chinese community know that these fundraising efforts would soon be expanded for another purpose.

• • •

World War Two, 1939–1945

In 1939 the world was plunged into another global war by Adolf Hitler, the leader of Nazi Germany. His invasion of Poland catapulted France, Britain, Canada, and other Commonwealth countries into war. At first Western Europe was the battleground. This changed when Germany's ally, Japan, invaded China in 1937 and, later, much of Southeast Asia. The battle zone of World War Two expanded to include both Europe and Asia.

Almost overnight the ten dire years of the Great Depression came to abrupt end. Thousands of able-bodied men who had been out of work joined the armed forces or had their pick of jobs in the war industry. Instead of making stoves, washing machines, and dryers, factories were converted to make guns, munitions, explosives, aircraft, military vehicles, and other machines of war. Even Casa Loma was converted, becoming a top secret location for making anti-submarine weapons.

Ronny Jaques/National Film Board of Canada/Library and Archives Canada.

In this photo from 1944, a munitions worker completes the assembly of a rifle at the John Inglis Company plant in Toronto.

Everybody, in their own way, contributed to the war effort. Not only did men and women go overseas to fight the war, the families left behind did their part. As men left their factory jobs to join the armed services, women stepped in to take over their jobs. For many it was their first chance to work outside the home and to take on responsibilities other than those of child-rearing and housecleaning. They soon excelled at such historically male-dominated trades as welding, ship-building, and engine repair. Without a doubt Canada's war production would not have been sustainable without women workers.

Stay-at-home women knitted sweaters, socks, and mitts for the soldiers. Pots and pans were donated for recycling into steel. Children collected bicycles, scrap metal, and clothes hangers: anything that could be melted down to make guns and ammunition. Even tin foil was saved from chewing gum and candy wrappers. Every bit, no matter how small, made a difference.

With food being shipped overseas to feed Canadian soldiers, shortages led to rationing, a strictly controlled limit allowed for each person. Families were mailed war ration books with weekly stamps and coupons for specific foods such as sugar and butter (250 grams, or a half pound), coffee (115 grams, or four ounces), tea (thirty grams, or one ounce), and meat (one kilogram, or two pounds). Gasoline was rationed so that this valuable fuel could be sent overseas for the military vehicles.

At the beginning of the war, the United States was neutral. However, Japan's surprise bombing of Pearl Harbor in Hawaii on December 7, 1941, resulted in a declaration of war against the Japanese, not only by the United States but also by Canada.

Less than eight hours after Pearl Harbour, the Japanese attacked and occupied Hong Kong, which was valiantly defended by two Canadian battalions, the Royal Rifles of Canada and the Winnipeg Grenadiers. It was hopeless from the start but the Canadian soldiers fought without letting up for eighteen days. Their defeat on December 25, 1941, remembered as Black Christmas, began a forty-four-month ordeal in Japanese prison camps for those captured. A total of 263 Canadians died in the battle, and 294 in captivity.

• • •

I'm Chinese

For the first time, Chinese Canadians were united with their fellow Canadians against a common enemy — Japan. Many Chinese Canadians wore handmade badges declaring, "I'm Chinese," so they wouldn't be mistaken as Japanese and bullied. They worked together with other Canadians to raise money to send to the armed forces. Purchasing more than any other group in Canada, the Chinese bought ten million dollars of Victory bonds that were sold by the Canadian government to raise money to fight the war.

• • •

Behind Enemy Lines

At the outbreak of the war, Canadian men and women served in the army on a voluntary basis. Prime Minister William Lyon Mackenzie King assured Canadians that no one would have to fight overseas unless they volunteered. By 1940, however, Germany had defeated France and occupied most of Western Europe. Britain was suddenly threatened with invasion, and more soldiers were desperately needed. As a result eligible Canadians were conscripted, that is, they were ordered by law to join the army.

The Chinese were excluded from conscription because they were considered a security risk. The governments in British Columbia and Saskatchewan were strongly against the Chinese being recruited because the right to vote would certainly become a demand after the war. Despite this exclusion many Chinese men and women volunteered to join the military because they wanted to prove their patriotism to Canada. They also wanted to fight the Japanese, who had occupied China and Hong Kong.

Things changed in 1944, when the British government asked for Chinese-Canadian recruits to be trained as spies against the Japanese. For the first time in Canada, being Chinese was an asset, not a liability. A secret mission was established, under the code name, "Operation Oblivion," to sabotage, demolish, infiltrate, and spy on the Japanese behind enemy lines. The chance of survival was slim; the military estimated that there would be an 80 percent casualty rate. The code name *Oblivion* had a very real meaning for those who took part in the mission — there was little to no chance of coming out alive. Participating meant near-certain death.

Nevertheless, more than one hundred Chinese Canadians volunteered for this dangerous mission. The Chinese community questioned their volunteerism. As one Chinese-Canadian war veteran remembered: "We had to stand up and face the room full of young people and their parents questioning us. 'What are the benefits? What are we going to get out of this? Who is going to guarantee us we are going to be treated as Canadians?'"[3]

Despite these objections, these brave volunteer recruits felt that this was something they had to do — stand shoulder-to-shoulder with their Canadian schoolmates. They underwent rigorous training in hand-to-hand combat, demolition, and other guerrilla warfare tactics. Every man had a suicide pill in case he was captured by the Japanese. The team was readied for action; however, a few weeks before the scheduled departure date, the mission was called off. The war was over.

After six years of devastating destruction, and the loss of fifty million lives, World War Two ended in Europe on May 8, 1945, called VE (Victory in Europe) Day. Celebrations spilled onto the streets as Torontonians danced, kissed strangers, and waved flags. The streetcars clanged their bells; cars honked their horns; church bells rang across the city.

Chinese-Canadian soldiers, pictured here on November 22, 1945, were stationed at Tweedsmuir Camp, England, to wait for their trip back home after the war..

Sgt. Karen M. Hermiston/Canada. Dept. of National Defence/Library and Archives Canada/PA-211879.

Three months later, on August 15, VJ (Victory in Japan) Day was declared. The war in the Pacific ended with the Americans dropping atomic bombs on the Japanese cities of Hiroshima and Nagasaki. No celebrations were louder than the ones in Chinatown. The country that had invaded and occupied China and Hong Kong was now defeated. Thousands of people filled Chinatown on Elizabeth Street to celebrate with loud music, lively lion dances, spectacular fireworks, and a grand parade that was later organized by the Chinese community.

JULY 6, 1945
BARKER AIRPORT
TORONTO, ONTARIO

Central Airways

Robert Wong Collection.

Brothers Robert (in cockpit) and Tommy Wong give a tour of one of their Central Airways airplanes to E.C. Mark (right) and Chong Ying (left), prominent leaders of Toronto's Chinese community.

• • •

Profile

Brothers Robert and Tommy Wong joined the Canadian Air Force. Their love of flying started at an early age when they were growing up. The two teenagers built a small airplane with a used car engine, based on drawings from a *Popular Mechanics* magazine. Construction started in the family's apartment in Chinatown, moved outdoors to the laneway, and finally to an airport for the final assembly. Their mother, her lady friends, and a younger sister sewed fabric to cover the wood frame. On a clear and sunny day in 1937, the plane, named the *Sky Scout*, flew its first flight. For Robert, "it was fun, exciting, and education, all in one."[4] After the war the Wong brothers opened a flying school called Central Airways on the Toronto Island.

War Brides

While thousands of Canadian troops were in Europe, many soldiers, some of them teenagers, met local girls, fell in love, and married. One of every five Canadian servicemen who went overseas as a bachelor came home a married man. When the war ended, however, they had to leave behind their war brides and return home with the troops. Within a short time, the Canadian government made arrangements for the war brides to come into the country — more than forty-eight thousand women arrived from England, Scotland, Wales, France, Belgium, Holland, and Italy. They didn't come alone; twenty-two thousand children, many of them born aboard ship, accompanied their mothers across the ocean to join their fathers.

Not included in the shiploads of women and children was the war bride of a Chinese Canadian — Sergeant George Thomas (Tom) Lock. While overseas in service for the Special Forces Unit, he married Joan Lim On, a Chinese-Australian girl. The dilemma was this. She wasn't allowed to come to Canada with the other war brides because of the Chinese Exclusion Act. Lock couldn't stay

Lock Family Collection.

Sergeant George Thomas (Tom) Lock and Joan Lim On on their wedding day in 1945. Her gown was made by her mother, a dressmaker.

with her in Australia because of her country's whites-only immigration policy. Eventually, she was given special permission by the Canadian government to come into Canada.

• • •

Light at the End of the Tunnel

Upon their return home, the war veterans were given many benefits to help them readjust to civilian life. They each received one hundred dollars to buy clothes, as well as an average lump sum of $488, based on length of service. Farm land was set aside for the returning soldiers to purchase at low prices. New, affordable houses, usually bungalows, were sold with loans at reasonable interest rates. They could also apply to get money to start a business, go to school, or attend university.

Compared to what the veterans of World War One had received, these benefits were much improved. Canadians who would never otherwise have had the chance to go to university were now able to do so with the government's financial support. War veteran Tom Lock, whose Australian wife was granted special entry into Canada, took advantage by enrolling in university. He graduated from the University of Toronto as its first Chinese-Canadian pharmacist and opened the first Chinese pharmacy in Toronto's Chinatown in 1954.

After the war fifty countries came together to establish the United Nations, which went on to proclaim the Universal Declaration of Human Rights in 1948. Since then, certain rights, including the right to life, liberty, equality before the law, and freedom of movement and thought, have been upheld. With the end of the war and the promising work of the United Nations on human rights, the Chinese community sensed a light at the end of what had been a long and dark tunnel. There was the hope that always comes with the birth of a new era.

SIX

Post-War Years

In large part due to the outcome of World War Two, the infamous Chinese Exclusion Act was repealed in 1947. In the twenty-four years since Humiliation Day in 1923, less than fifty Chinese had come into Canada under the exempted status of diplomats, merchants, and students. During those years many things had happened that affected the attitudes and perceptions in Canada about Chinese Canadians:

- Six hundred Chinese-Canadian men and women served as soldiers, pilots, nurses, and cadets in Canada's army, air force, and navy;
- Chinese Canadians worked in wartime shipyards and factories;
- Chinese Canadians raised millions of dollars for the Victory bond drive;
- Chinese Canadians worked side by side with other Canadians in aid agencies, like the Red Cross;

- China and Canada were allies during the war;
- Canada appointed its first ambassador to China in 1943;
- The United States repealed its Exclusion Act in 1943;
- Canada's Chinese Exclusion Act was deemed to contravene the United Nations Charter of Human Rights.

Following World War Two, the Chinese gained a higher level of acceptance, one never before experienced. They had proven their loyalty to Canada during the war. Canadians realized that Chinese-Canadian sons and daughters, like their own children, had put their lives on the line for their country, and, slowly, acceptance was extended to them.

• • •

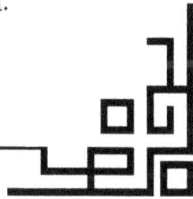

The Vote

Something else to celebrate was the gaining of the right to vote. Up until 1947 the law excluded the Chinese from voting in the federal elections across Canada and in provincial elections in British Columbia and Saskatchewan. Anyone who wanted to be a pharmacist, doctor, lawyer, or enter any other profession in these two provinces was barred because being on the voting list was a requirement.

This all changed in 1947 when Chinese Canadians all across Canada gained full provincial and federal voting rights. The right to vote did not come easily. Other immigrants had gained it immediately when they became citizens, but Chinese Canadians were granted it only after they had fought and sacrificed their lives in two world wars. The vote was a fundamental right and cornerstone of democracy, and Chinese Canadians finally had a political voice to make a difference.

• • •

Family Reunification

The end of the Chinese Exclusion Act should have been a happy occasion for Chinese families, but it wasn't. Chinese Canadians could sponsor their wives, children, and parents to come to Canada, but this special program for family reunification had many restrictions.

Did You Know?

Until 1947 Canadians were British subjects living in Canada, not Canadian citizens. The Chinese, even if they were born in Canada, were classified as aliens, who could become British subjects only by applying for citizenship. They had to appear before a judge, who decided if the applicant would make a good citizen. More often than not, Chinese applicants were rejected because they were considered unsuitable.

In 1947 citizenship was granted to all eligible Canadians, whether or not they had been born in Canada. Canada was the first Commonwealth country to have its own citizenship, distinct and apart from that of Great Britain. Canadians finally became Canadian citizens.

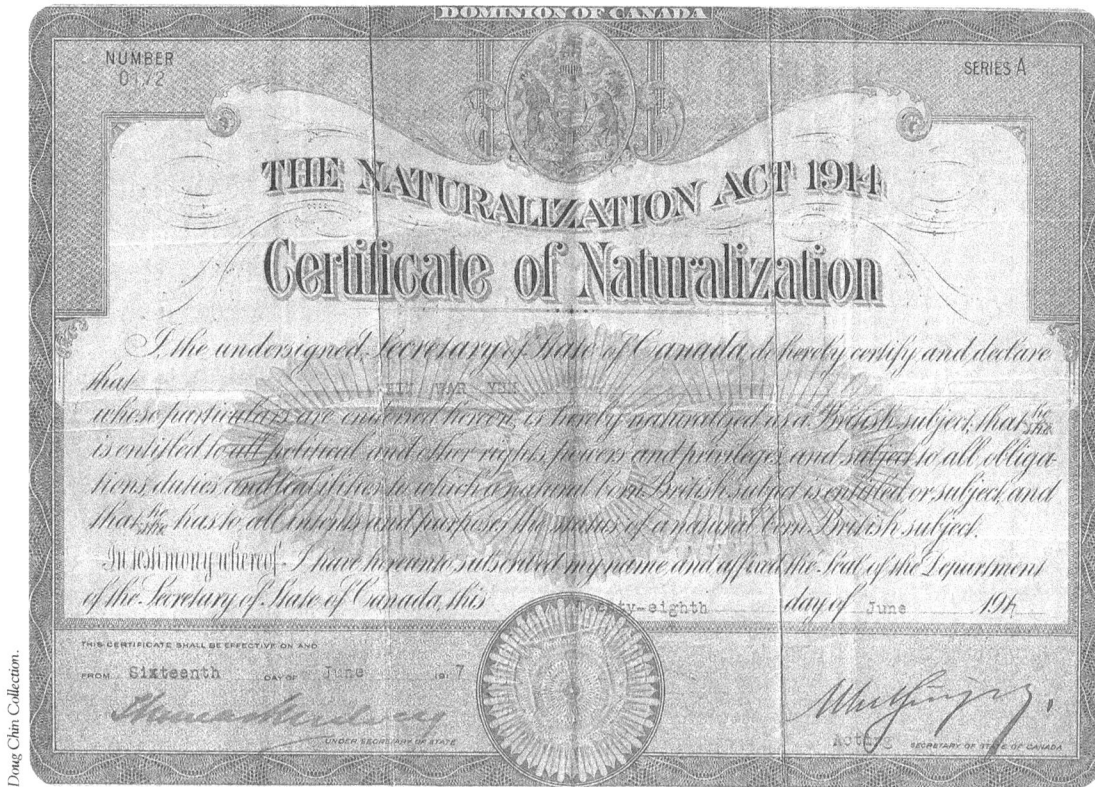

Doug Chin Collection.

This 1922 document shows that Hin War Yum was a British citizen. He was one of the few Chinese who was successful in his application for citizenship.

The problem was this: only Chinese who had become British subjects could apply to bring their families from China. Of the 34,627 Chinese in Canada, only 2,055, less than 5 percent, were British subjects. Additionally, there were many strict eligibility requirements. For example, children had to be under the age of eighteen. This meant that adult children could not be sponsored. So, rather than being excited about the possibility of being reunited with their families, the Chinese had to look with envy at the post-war newcomers flowing in from Europe and the United States. There were no restrictions for them. Clearly, white immigrants still held a privileged position for entry to Canada.

• • •

Who Is This Person?

The arrival of eligible Chinese wives and children began as a trickle, and the stories of these early family reunifications were heart-wrenching. After years of separation, family members found it difficult reacquainting themselves with each other and adjusting to their new circumstances. There were cases of husbands and wives who had not seen each other for over twenty years. Children, who had been born after their fathers returned to Canada from their brief visits in China, were introduced to complete strangers they had to call "Father."

Many children were already adults, as was the case for the son of Lee Chang. His mother remembered: "We were married in 1935. I was nineteen then. The next year Melvin was born. We stayed in China while we waited to come. Finally, we came in 1955. Melvin was twenty-one when he met his father for the first time."[1]

Profile

Stanley Woo arrived from Hong Kong in 1950 after the repeal of the Chinese Exclusion Act. He was sponsored by his father, who owned a grocery store, Millwood Produce, in Leaside. His father later entered into a partnership with Dr. Henry Lore and others to open the Won Way Restaurant at 126 Elizabeth Street in Chinatown. Dr. Woo attended Northern Secondary School, then the University of Toronto, where he was the first student born in China to graduate from its medical school.

Poy Tong was a teenager when he was reunited with his father. Their relationship suffered because of the prolonged separation of twelve years. He remembered thinking, "Who is this person? He's my dad, yet I don't know him."[2]

In other cases single men, now in their late forties, returned to their villages in China to find a wife, often choosing ones twenty to thirty years younger than them. Within a short time of the newly wedded couples' arrival in Canada, children would be born. It was not unusual to see a family where the husband was an older man, the wife was a young woman who looked more like the husband's daughter, and the young children looked more like the father's grandchildren.

After some husbands and wives were reunited, they had children born to them in their older years. One young girl from Toronto remembered: "My grandparents were already in their forties when my father was born. My grandmother was forty-seven years old when she had her last child. Did you know that my father's sister is twenty-one years older than my father? And that he is younger than his own nephew, and that I have a niece who is thirteen years old? Well, it is all because of the Chinese Head Tax and the Chinese Exclusion Act."[3]

• • •

Profile

Jean Lumb was born in Nanaimo, British Columbia, in 1919. She was one of twelve children. During the Great Depression, her father couldn't find enough work to feed her and the rest of the family. When she was twelve years old, she faced terrible news from her father. She was told that she had to quit school to work to make money for her family. "I cried that night because I was just beginning to enjoy and appreciate my new school in Vancouver."[4] Even with her job, not enough money was made, so she moved to Toronto in 1935 as a sixteen-year-old to work at her married sister's restaurant. By age eighteen she had opened her own grocery store.

When she arrived in the city, she noticed all of the lonely men in Chinatown living without their wives and children; they left a lasting impression on her. She became a champion for changing Canada's immigration laws that kept families separated. For her community activism, she was the first Chinese-Canadian woman to receive the Order of Canada.

Jean Lumb Collection.

In 1957 a delegation of community leaders, the only woman being Jean Lumb, met with Prime Minister John Diefenbaker to convince the Canadian government to change the immigration laws that separated families.

Paper Sons and Daughters

For others who couldn't sponsor their children, desperate times called for desperate measures. They got around the system by paying for illegal documents: false identity papers. Take, for example, the situation of a son who was over the age of eighteen. He was too old to be sponsored, so his father bought a document from another family, who had a son under the age of eighteen. The son entered the country as a "paper son" because he was only real "on paper."

Children, both paper sons and paper daughters, came to Canada with false names and identities. They pretended to be somebody else, using the name of another person and playing the part of being a member of another family. A Wong became a Chan or a Mark became a Lee, just like that. These children lived their lives in silent fear of being discovered and deported. They had to keep up the lie about their age, surnames, and their parents.

The Canadian government came to realize that something needed to change. In 1960 the Chinese Adjustment Program was established to allow illegal Chinese immigrants to come forward and apply for legal status without fear of being sent back to Hong Kong and China. The scheme of illegal paper sons and paper daughters soon came to end.

• • •

The Cold War

While Canada tackled its immigration challenges, post-war events were changing world politics. Britain's days as a great power did not survive after World War Two. Not only had terrible bombings devastated the country, but the cost of war had emptied its treasury. These economic changes combined with changes in the political world, such as rising nationalism in the colonies, prompted Britain, along with France and Portugal, to withdraw from their colonies in Africa and Asia. Among the colonies that gained their independence following the war, several were of particular significance for China, such as Hong Kong, Vietnam, and Macau. The retreat of the Western powers from these colonies would eventually allow for the emergence of China as a power in Asia.

In the early days following World War Two, however, China was still poor and weak. The United States, on the other hand, emerged as the most powerful and prosperous post-war country. Unlike the war-torn countries of Europe, all of which had been devastated by the war, it only became stronger economically.

That economic strength was offset, however, by a military threat. The United States had developed the nuclear bomb, but shortly after the war the Soviet Union stole the secret and built its own bomb. Although the United States and the Soviet Union had fought side by side against the Nazis during the war, their relationship afterwards was rocky, at best. Both sides distrusted the other. The 1950s became a fearful time.

Tension between the two superpowers escalated, and the era known as the Cold War began. The Cold War would dominate world affairs for decades. Many major crises arose during that time, over hotspots such as Cuba, Korea, Vietnam, and, in particular, the Berlin Wall, which became a symbol of the hostility between the East and the West.

What was feared in the Western world was that Communism would spread, and that the democratic and capitalist systems in the free world, including Canada, would fall. Communism became a dirty word, and anyone with Communist leanings or sympathies were looked upon with great suspicion.

For forty years the United States and the Soviet Union pointed missiles at each other's strategic sites and threatened nuclear war at the push of a button. Spies kept watch on both sides. This precarious state of affairs lasted until 1991, when the Berlin Wall that separated West and East Germany came tumbling down. Communist regimes in Eastern Europe fell, and the Soviet Union dissolved into independent republics, thereby ending the era of the Cold War. Communism, however, was not without a country.

• • •

One China Too Many

The Soviet Union wasn't the only Communist country that caused the West concern after World War Two. On October 10, 1949, the People's Republic of China was established as the new China by Communist leader, Mao Zedong. "The Chinese people have stood up!" he declared. By this time China bore little resemblance to the China of old. The country was broken and battered by decades of civil war, occupation by Western countries, famines, and war with Japan.

When the People's Republic of China was established in 1949, the defeated Nationalist Party (Guomindang) and two million supporters fled across the Taiwan Strait to Taiwan, an island located sixty kilometres from mainland China. There, Chiang Kai-shek, who ruled as president from 1949 until his death in 1975, established the Republic of China with Taipei as its capital city. He found strong support from anti-Communist groups, especially the overseas Chinese in Canada.

For the next twenty or so years, Taiwan was recognized as the one and only China. However, Taiwan experienced a gradual loss of diplomatic and political presence in international politics. In 1971 the United Nations expelled Taiwan and recognized the People's Republic of China as the legitimate China.

To this day mainland China maintains there is only one China, which it claims includes Taiwan, and opposes any support for "one China, one Taiwan" or "two Chinas." Taiwan, on the other hand, regards the government in China as illegitimate and claims that the mainland rightfully belongs to Taiwan.

In Toronto the birth of a new China under Mao Zedong had a major impact on the Chinese community. There were now two Chinas: the People's Republic of China, under Communist rule; and the Republic of China, under the Nationalist Party. The existence of two Chinas split the Chinese community in Toronto into two factions — pro-Communist and anti-Communist. Strongly divided loyalties remain to this day.

TABLE 1: Two Chinas

	People's Republic of China	Republic of China
Also Known As	China; mainland China	Taiwan
Population	1.3 billion	23 million
Capital	Beijing	Taipei
Official Language	Mandarin	Mandarin
Territory	10 million kilometres^2	35,980 kilometres^2
Government	Communist	Democratic
National Holiday	October 1	October 10
National flag		

More important than the political differences this division caused amongst the Chinese in Toronto, however, was their concern all felt for the safety and well-being of their families in China. Many people had fled to Hong Kong; some went missing during the civil war leading up to the revolution in 1949. The Chinese in Toronto anxiously read the newspapers for updates about what was happening there. At least two-thirds of the families in the province of Guangdong depended on financial help from their overseas relatives, and there was no way to make sure that their relatives were receiving the money being sent to them. Once the new Communist government was established in 1949, China shut itself from the rest of the world. No one was allowed to leave or visit China, and no more money could be sent.

The Communist government implemented drastic changes to restore China to its former glory. Following the beliefs of Communist doctrine, Mao Zedong banned religion and private business. He also sought to undermine anyone who held an elevated position in the country, and so the families of immigrants who had prospered from the hard-earned savings sent to them from Canada were terrorized, tortured, and humiliated. Their homes, farms, and possessions were confiscated. All landowners were labelled enemies of the people and forced to give up their property for the newly organized communes, which were made up of the farms taken from them and peasant farmers. Every aspect of life was controlled and owned by the communes.

The old and traditional ways of life were declared bad influences during the Cultural Revolution (1966–1976). Thousands of teachers, writers, government officials, and politicians were branded as enemies of the people and punished as traitors. Museums, libraries, and temples were destroyed. The situation was not better for the masses of peasants, who died by the millions from widespread famines caused by disastrous government campaigns like the Cultural Revolution.

Millions were forced into hard labour and tens of thousands were executed. The country remained poor and backward, and its citizens were persecuted if they questioned anything. There were no outcomes of the Communist government's campaigns that merited celebration — such a sharp contrast to life in Canada. The country was flourishing and its citizens were prospering. As the centennial anniversary of its founding approached, Canada planned a national celebration for Canadians and visitors alike in 1967.

Profile

Eddie Ing's grandfather paid the one hundred dollar head tax in 1901. He lived for fifty years without his family, who remained in China. During World War Two, he worked as a cook and housekeeper for a wealthy lawyer and sent his savings to his wife and son. After the Communist government was established in 1949, his son and daughter-in-law were jailed for five years. Their crime was being landowners, at the time labelled as enemies of the people.

Their son, Eddie Ing, escaped to Hong Kong and came to Canada in 1954. At his first job, he worked eighteen hours a day, seven days a week, and earned twenty-five cents an hour in a Toronto Chinese restaurant. In 1955 he opened up his own Chinese restaurant in Chinatown.[5]

Happy 100th Birthday

The year 1967 was a time for celebration: Canada was one hundred years old. Centennial parties started on January 1 and lasted for the entire year from coast to coast. A nation of twenty million at the time, Canada enjoyed one of the highest standards of living in the world. The nation was blossoming and coming into its own as a country, redefining its identity as something unique from that of Great Britain and the United States.

The centennial was not the only reason for celebration that year. The Chinese community was overjoyed when the country's immigration laws were overhauled. Two decades after the repeal of the Chinese Exclusion Act, nationality and race were finally removed as discriminatory restrictions on immigration.

Based on a new assessment system, points were assigned to applicants for age, education, ability to speak English or French, and the need for their skills. In short, immigrants who could contribute to Canadian society were encouraged to come. For the first time since 1885, the Chinese were on an equal footing with all other immigrants applying to

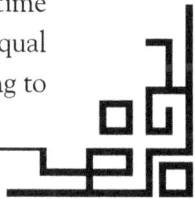

come into Canada. This major change of the immigration system drastically altered the face of the Chinese community in Canada.

Canada became even more popular, the choice destination for immigrants, when multiculturalism was introduced by Prime Minister Pierre Trudeau in 1971. The first country to have such a policy, Canada wanted to be a nation where all of its citizens, regardless of their different backgrounds, would be respected and treated equally and where diverse cultures would exist side by side in harmony. Since then other changes in government policy have helped to make Canada even more appealing. The Canadian Charter of Rights and Freedoms, instituted in 1982, guarantees every citizen freedom in religion, thought, and expression. With all of these changes, Canada has attracted new citizens from all over the world — including many more from Asia.

• • •

Hong Kong

Waves of Chinese immigrants arrived, first from Hong Kong. Although this British colony occupied a mere one thousand square kilometres of space — it was little more than a rock in the ocean — it had established itself as a pow-

erful trading and financial centre. Hong Kong had been heavily battered by World War Two; the Japanese occupation had nearly destroyed the city, and its citizens endured years of violence and food shortages. However, post-war recovery was rapid, and within a short time, Hong Kong exploded with economic growth. Office towers and condominiums soon dotted the skyline; malls and restaurants filled the crowded streets. With these successes the rich got richer and the poor got poorer. Most of the poor people were refugees from China.

Hong Kong had been the destination for refugees from China for many years. At first, it was the Sino-Japanese War that pushed the Chinese out of China into Hong Kong. More unrest followed during the civil war between the Nationalist government and the Chinese Communists. Then, hundreds of thousands of people escaped to Hong Kong just before and after 1949, the year that the People's Republic of China was established. Untold numbers fled from Communism by all means possible — by boat, by foot, and by swimming.

Soon, Hong Kong was bursting at the seams with refugees. Over three hundred thousand of them lived with their pigs, chickens, and ducks on its slopes and ravines in makeshift huts assembled out of boards and pieces of tin. Desperate as they were to find a welcoming place, the options were limited. Taiwan refused them. Australia's doors were closed to Chinese immigrants. The United States accepted a limited number. Canada, on the other hand, gradually accepted more and more immigrants from Hong Kong because refugees were given special consideration for entry.

Profile

Vivienne Poy was the first Asian Canadian appointed to the Senate of Canada. Her life has not always been easy, however. She was born in Hong Kong at a time of war, and has first-hand knowledge of the refugee experience. When she was a baby, her family fled to China to escape the Japanese occupation of Hong Kong. For years they lived on the move as refugees, selling her mother's jewels in order to survive, and eating a diet made up almost exclusively of hard-boiled eggs. "To this day I hate them," she remembers. "I'll always remember the smell, the taste."[6]

In 1967, riots organized by pro-Communist supporters ripped through Hong Kong to protest British rule. There soon followed further demonstrations, as well as acts of terror, assassinations, bombings, and other acts of violence. The British mobilized twelve thousand police and ten thousand soldiers to regain law and order.[7] This unrest closed businesses. Factories shut down and moved elsewhere, to countries such as Taiwan and South Korea. Tourism, the British colony's second largest money-maker, dropped to an all-time low as travellers stayed away. The riots forced its citizens to face the unpleasant reality that there was a danger of a Communist takeover in their future, and, not surprisingly, a mass exit from Hong Kong began. Visa applications to countries, including Canada, shot up by 300 percent.

• • •

One Country, Two Systems

In 1984 China and Britain came to an agreement: Hong Kong would be handed back to China when Britain's ninety-nine-year lease on the territory expired in 1997.

What did this mean? It meant a lot for residents in Hong Kong, who were accustomed to a Western-style, democratic government.

The thought of suddenly becoming citizens of a Communist country was frightening, especially for business people.

The terms of the handover were simple. China agreed that Hong Kong would keep its democratic government and successful economic system for fifty years following the transfer, operating as a Special Administrative Region of China — in its words, "One country, two systems." People in the British colony, however, were very nervous because they didn't trust China's commitment to the conditions of the handover. The number of people exiting Hong Kong tripled after the announcement of the impending handover.

As if to show how bad things might be, the unimaginable happened in 1989. The world watched in disbelief as events unfolded in Tiananmen Square, the world's largest public square, in Beijing. A large group of students held a hunger strike. The demonstration grew to more than a million people, easily the largest pro-democracy event in China's history. They were joined by supporters around the world, including thirty thousand who gathered at Toronto's city hall in the city's largest rally ever for an international event.

In China the authorities struck back. The ferocity and violence of the attack on the peaceful protest by the Chinese army shocked the world. Tanks rolled onto the square, an event that was vividly described by Canadian journalist Jan Wong, who was a witness from her hotel room overlooking the square. "They used tanks … [and] they plowed over people. If you were in their way, they would just run over you. The tanks are incredibly heavy, so heavy they leave an imprint on the asphalt. They just go over it, and there's the tank tread. That's how much they weigh." Gunshots were fired without warning. "There were many, many wounded and dead that night because they kept firing into the crowds."[8] Terrified people ran in all directions, leaving bodies strewn on the pavement. Untold numbers of civilians were killed by gunfire, trampled to death, or crushed under military vehicles.

Not surprisingly, the confidence of the people in Hong Kong was shaken. This forceful display of control and oppression painted a realistic picture of what could happen after Britain's handover to China in 1997. When Canada introduced new immigration laws to encourage business people who had a minimum of five hundred thousand dollars to invest in 1986, the exodus of people leaving the British colony reached record heights and peaked at forty-four thousand in 1994. Hong

Kong became Canada's top source of immigrants — well-educated, English-speaking people, they settled and adapted with more ease than many other immigrants.

• • •

Indochina

A second wave of immigrants arrived in Canada from Vietnam. In 1959 Vietnam was a country split into two, with a Communist government in the north and a democratic government in the south. A civil war waged for over fifteen years as each half fought to create one unified nation based on its system. The Vietnam War ended in 1975 with the victory of North Vietnam and Communism. Freedom was taken away from the South Vietnamese and human rights vanished. People lived in constant fear of arrest and abuse by the Communists so they fled by the thousands.

Within a short time, they were joined by refugees from other Indochinese countries — Cambodia and Laos. Over one million Indochinese risked their lives to escape war and persecution by any means possible, even when the only means of escape was a dangerous journey in an unseaworthy boat. The people who fled in such boats became known as "boat people"; they spent days afloat at sea under threat of drowning in huge waves or attack by pirates.

From 1979 to 1981, Canada sponsored 60,049 Indochinese refugees, a third of them ethnic Chinese.[9] For opening its doors, Canada was honoured in 1986 by the United Nations for the "remarkable achievement of individuals, families, voluntary agencies, community and religious organizations, as well as federal, provincial and municipal authorities in helping refugees to integrate successfully into Canadian society and regain human dignity."[10]

Among the newcomers were two refugee children who arrived in Ontario in 1979. A fifteen-year-old girl and her ten-year-old brother, they had faced the worst dangers before their safe arrival. They were crammed with over five hundred other passengers on a small boat from Saigon to Malaysia. During the five-day journey, pirates attacked no less than six times. During one attack their boat was rammed, and two men, one armed with a knife and the other with a screwdriver, robbed all of the passengers. The children had to give up a wristwatch that belonged to their father and a jade necklace that belonged to their mother. They eventually made it to safety, however.[11] Their first impression of Ontario? They were amazed and stunned by the cold and the snow.

Timothy Tran, another refugee, remembered arriving in Toronto as one of the boat people. His parents had died in Vietnam. "I fled with my four brothers and one sister by boat in 1979. I was fifteen. We spent four days and three nights on the South China Sea, then arrived hungry and penniless in Malaysia. The United Nations High Commissioner for Refugees granted us status as political refugees, interviewed my family, and agreed to resettle us in Canada."[12]

• • •

Republic of China (Taiwan)

Another wave of immigrants arrived from Taiwan starting in the late 1970s. By this time the founding leader, Chiang Kai-shek, had died, and the country was on the road to changing its government. Although Taiwan's economy was prospering and was one of the strongest in East Asia, there was great unrest. Protesters were demanding democracy and an end to martial law.

Eventually, these protests bore fruit. A more democratic society began to develop, and in 1987 there was an end to martial law. The growing economy needed skilled workers and created a higher standard of living, two incentives for the Taiwanese to stay in their country. As a result, immigration of people from Taiwan to Canada slowed in the 1980s.

The 1990s and the early 2000s, however, have been troubling times for the Taiwanese. Just as the Tiananmen Square incident in Beijing spurred a sudden exodus of Hong Kong residents, the increasingly rocky relationship between Taiwan and China has lately led more people from Taiwan to want to leave. They believe that their country will one day be reclaimed by China. Although relations between the two Chinas have become more relaxed, with increased trade, and cultural and educational exchanges, anxious Taiwanese have moved away in large numbers, mostly to the United States, Australia, and also Canada (see Table 2). Vancouver is the first choice for the majority of Taiwanese immigrants, followed by Toronto.

TABLE 2: Immigration from Taiwan to Canada

1981–1990	11,275
1991–2000	41,820
2001–2006	10,726

Source: Census Canada

• • •

People's Republic of China

The most recent wave of Chinese immigrants has come from China. A milestone in the history of Chinese immigration was reached in 1970 when an agreement between China and Canada allowed Chinese Canadians to sponsor their families. Within a few years, the increase of people leaving China for Canada was dramatic, jumping from two thousand in 1971 to fifty-five thousand in 1973. The Chinese community blossomed with reunited families, such a positive change from the days of the Chinese Exclusion Act when there were so few women and children. The bachelor society days were finally over.

Family reunification was in large part due to the strongly developing relationship between China and Canada. Under the leadership of Prime Minister Pierre Elliott Trudeau, Canada was one of the first Western countries to recognize China, doing so in 1970. He was the first Canadian prime minister to pay an official visit to China, thereby laying the foundation for the subsequent growth in Canada-China relations that continues to this day.

Did You Know?

Panda bears have been symbols of Chinese goodwill and diplomacy from as far back as the seventh century, when the empress gave a pair of pandas to Japan. In 1972 two pandas were gifted to the United States after President Nixon's historic visit to Beijing. In 1985 Pandamania swept the Toronto Zoo when it was the short-term home of two giant pandas, a significant diplomatic gesture by the Chinese government. Beginning in 2013, two pandas will spend five years at the Toronto Zoo as a "friendly" loan from China.

Another change had an even more significant impact on Chinese immigration to Canada than the family reunification program — the opening of China's doors for its people to leave the country. After the Communist takeover in 1949, emigration was strictly controlled, and very few could leave. In 1985 China allowed its citizens to apply for emigration, and thousands chose Canada as their destination.

Why do so many Chinese want to leave China? One reason is the one-child policy that was implemented in 1979 to control the population, then fast approaching one billion people. With few exceptions families have been allowed to have only one child. Of course this has had a big impact on Chinese families. Children have no brothers or sisters. Parents have only one child who will look after them in their old age. By coming to Canada, families can have as many children as they want.

The second reason for the exodus from China is that Canada is seen as promising a more certain future, particularly for business people. After the death of Mao Zedong in 1976, the new leader, Deng Xiaoping, introduced dramatic changes that have made China one of the greatest success stories in the economic world. However, the biggest risk for businesses there is the fact that the Communist Party that can take away anyone's wealth at the snap of a finger. No law protects the individual business owner.

And the last and final reason for the growing ranks of Chinese leaving China is the unrest of its citizens. There is dissatisfaction with

> ## Profile
>
> "I came to Canada with my husband in 2000 from Guangzhou, in China. In general we had a good living there…. We wanted a country that could give us more fairness, more equality. Because we cannot communicate in English as fluently as we can in Chinese, we cannot get the same jobs as we had in China. However, we accept this change. We now have a Canadian-born daughter who will get the benefit from the education system here, and we hope she will have a much better future than us."[13]
>
> ~Rena Yang

the school system and health care. Freedom of speech, freedom of the press, and religious freedoms — basic rights that are often taken for granted in Canada — are not guaranteed.

For all of these reasons, Chinese immigrants, an average of 33,443 each year, have applied to come to Canada. From 1996 to 2006, China replaced Hong Kong as the largest source of immigrants to Canada.[14]

SEVEN

Toronto's Chinatowns

Where did all these waves of Chinese newcomers live when they arrived in Toronto? After the war Chinatown began rebuilding with the arrival of Chinese immigrants. At the same time, however, there were changes happening around the city — changes that would take a heavy toll on Chinatown. Land developers began tearing down thousands of houses and buildings: ten thousand between 1955 and 1965, and another eighteen thousand between 1965 and 1975.[1] These were replaced by office complexes, high-rise apartments, shopping centres, and parking lots, but the plans for a new city hall had the most devastating impact on Chinatown.

In 1947 Toronto's government approved a project, without any consultation with the Chinese community, to build a new city hall and public square on the land where Chinatown was located. The city had the right to expropriate land — that is, buy any private property that was to be used for public purpose. By 1958 two-thirds of Chinatown was expropriated. Businesses, homes, and other buildings were bulldozed to the ground and a four-year construction project began. In 1965, the same year that the new Canadian maple leaf flag was flown for the first time, the new city hall and Nathan Phillips Square were officially opened.

Now that the new city hall was built, the city wanted to take over more land from Chinatown. This time the Chinese community fought back and protested further development. In 1967 the Save Chinatown Committee, made up of leaders from Chinese organizations and led by Jean Lumb, presented their case to the city politicians. It was successful in saving what was left of Chinatown.

The construction of New City Hall in Toronto eventually required the demolition of the historic Land Registry building, the grounds of which were a popular play area for children.

TORONTO'S FIRST CHINATOWN
多倫多的首個唐人街

The first Chinese resident recorded in Toronto was Sam Ching, the owner of a hand laundry business on Adelaide Street in 1878. Though immigration to Canada directly from China was restricted after 1885, Ching was eventually joined by Chinese men who migrated from western Canada after helping to build the transcontinental Canadian Pacific Railway.

Between 1900 and 1925, Toronto's first Chinese community took shape here, around Elizabeth Street which once ran all the way south to Queen Street. 'Chinatown' was a bustling commercial and residential area that included restaurants, grocery stores, and traditional clan associations.

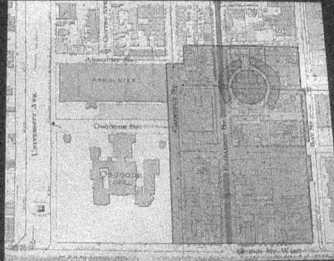

Detail of 1923 Goad's Fire Insurance Plan showing the streets of Toronto's first Chinatown. Chinatown's main street, Elizabeth Street, is coloured red. The area shaded in grey was demolished in the 1950s for Nathan Phillips Square and City Hall.
City of Toronto Archives; © CGI.

根據記載，多倫多的第一個華裔居民是 "Sam Ching"。一八七八年，他在 Adelaide 街經營洗衣店。一八八五年後，雖然加拿大政府限制華人從中國直接移居加國，但參與興建橫跨加拿大太平洋鐵路的華人在鐵路完成後，從加拿大西部移居多倫多，最終與 "Sam Ching" 一同居於此地。

在一九零零年至一九二五年之間，多倫多的第一個華人社區在伊麗莎白街一帶建立起來。伊麗莎白街一度向南伸延至皇后街。當時的 "唐人街" 是一個照來攘往的商業和住宅區，餐館、雜貨店和宗親會比比皆是。

戈德在一九二三年製作的火災保險圖顯示多倫多第一個唐人街的街道。紅色的是唐人街的主要街道伊麗莎白街。灰色的部分在五十年代拆毀，以興建藩教菲臘廣場和多倫多市政大樓。
多倫多市政府檔案室；© CGI

Jean Lumb Collection.

The original location of Toronto's Chinatown is marked with a plaque on Nathan Phillips Square.

Old Chinatown, as it is known today, stands as a shadow of its former self, no longer the bustling centre of the Chinese community. Rather, the few remaining restaurants and stores serve local office workers, tourists getting off the buses at the Bay Street bus terminal, or shoppers wandering over from the Eaton Centre a few blocks away.

• • •

Chinatown West

After most of Chinatown was demolished, Chinese businesses and residents were forced to move. Most went west along Dundas Street towards Spadina Avenue, less than one kilometre away. This area was once the centre of Irish, Jewish, Portuguese, and Italian immigrants; after these groups moved away, there was an established neighbourhood with homes and businesses ready to be purchased at less expensive prices than the properties the Chinese had been forced to leave in Old Chinatown. Where there had been stores such as Shopsy's Delicatessen, Sammy Taft World Famous Hatter, and Hyman's Book and Art Shop, the Chinese moved in with their restaurants, retail shops, bakeries, pharmacies, doctors' offices, and book stores. All

of the new businesses needed people, not only as customers but also as workers. The restaurants hired cooks, cleaners, busboys, and wait staff. The shops needed sales clerks. By 1971, homes on the side streets off Spadina Avenue were largely occupied by the Chinese. This area became known as Chinatown West.

Newcomers from Hong Kong, from the 1980s and onwards, brought in a lot of money, which was invested in all kinds of businesses. These were not the type of immigrants who wanted to open small family businesses such as laundries, cafés, and grocery stores. With their financial resources and experience, they invested heavily and revitalized Chinatown West with newer and bigger businesses. Many set up real estate businesses and offices providing professional services in medicine, law, and accounting. Restaurants were opened to seat not one hundred but one thousand diners. Famous chefs were brought in from Hong Kong to cook dishes that were vastly different from the ones that had been adapted by the early Chinese-Canadian restaurants to suit Canadian tastes. Within a short time, Chinese cuisine rivalled the food of Hong Kong.

Not only that, these newcomers formed a new Chinese-Canadian middle class, one with global connections, an entrepreneurial spirit, rich cultural values, and a collective voice on a scale not heard before about important community issues.

• • •

A Career Choice Out of No Choice

The south part of Chinatown West was once the centre of a thriving clothing industry, a rag trade where factories made clothing for the growing population in Toronto. In the 1920s the garment workers were mostly Italian, Greek, and other European men. After World War Two, these male workers moved into better paying jobs and were replaced by women, who laboured long hours with little pay and in terrible conditions.

The places where these women worked were sweatshops, literally, because everyone had to sweat for every meagre pennies that were earned. These jobs, however, provided work for newcomers who had limited skills and education, and no command of the English language.

Gradually, the Chinese took over these low-paying jobs. When these factories started closing down in the late 1980s, many workers were forced to start working at home, sewing for the finest and often most expensive clothing lines. They had to buy their own sewing machines, ones designed especially for industrial work so that they could do "piece work" from home. Instead of being paid an hourly rate, they were paid according to the number of garments or pieces from the garments.

Profile

One homeworker who came to Toronto from China spoke little English. She ended up working in garment factories. After three years of sewing and the birth of her first child in 1985, she set up a work area in her basement. She remembered, "It was very important for me to raise my own kids. But when I worked at home, I could only make about three dollars an hour. I tried to sew as much as I could once I had time, normally after my kids had fallen asleep. I would ask my husband to put the children to bed so I could work until very late at night. It was a career choice out of no choice."[2]

Imagine the hardship of these women. They had no one to socialize with, and worked alone at home without any benefits, like vacation and sick pay. When their children came home from school, meals had to be prepared. The women resumed their sewing into the late hours of the night. They put in these long hours to make as much money as possible because, more often than not, they earned less than minimum wage.

• • •

Fighting Back

It didn't take long before Chinatown West was faced with threats of development and land expropriation. There were a number of factors behind this threat:

- The University of Toronto planned on expanding its campus to Spadina Avenue;
- Ontario Hydro had plans to build a twelve-storey electrical transformer station;
- The Toronto Police Services wanted to build the 52 Division Police Station on Beverley Street;
- A land developer proposed a plan to build a large mall on Spadina Avenue;
- The Spadina Expressway was planned for extension into downtown Toronto.

The Chinese community rallied support from long-time residents, social workers, activists, as well as like-minded city politicians such as John Sewell, David Crombie, and William Kilbourn, who worked tirelessly to stop the bulldozers that were destroying the old neighbourhoods in Toronto.

Today Chinatown West is thriving. People crowd the sidewalks, some doing their shopping, others on their way to a restaurant. Stores and markets display their colourful fruit, assorted vegetables, dried herbs, t-shirts, handbags, and souvenirs, many spilling out on the sidewalks. Street vendors sell clothing, trinkets, and home-grown vegetables. Cars drive bumper to bumper in congested traffic clogged by delivery trucks that are double-parked as fresh meats, vegetables, and supplies are unloaded. The chatter is in Mandarin, Cantonese, Taishanese, Hakka, and Vietnamese. Family associations, such as the Lung Kong Kung So family association on Spadina Avenue, continue to provide a meeting place for their members. Restaurants lining the streets serve all manner of Chinese food; not only Cantonese food, as in the early years, but diverse and varied cuisines from Hunan, Shanghai, Vietnam, and Sichuan.

Jens Ronneberger.

The Dragon City mall features shopping on the first and second floors, professional offices on the third, and the Sky Dragon Restaurant at the top.

The largest malls are the Dragon City at the corner of Spadina Avenue and Dundas Street and Chinatown Centre, one block south. Shoes, clothes, books, DVDs, electronics, and jewellery are sold alongside tourist items such as silk slippers, fans, back scratchers, and incense. The ever-popular restaurants and food stalls there feature specialties, such as bubble tea, barbecued meats, and noodles.

A famous animal sculpture, named Lucky Moose, presides over Chinatown West. In 2000 326 life-sized moose appeared all around Toronto — on streets, front lawns, roof tops,

William Greer.

The dragon, phoenix, Monkey King, and unicorn were sculpted by Millie Chen and Warren Quigley to form the Chinese word meaning "gateway."

David Hlynsky and Shirley Yanover.

Shirley Yanover and David Hlynsky created this dragon sculpture for Chinatown West as a tribute to Chinese new-comers to Toronto.

and store balconies. Made of fibreglass and decorated in ways to match their locations or owners, these moose filled the city, making it, in the words of Mayor Mel Lastman, who had his own "Mel Moose" at City Hall, "the moose capital of the world." The moose event was planned as a tourist attraction to put Toronto on the world map, but it had another benefit:

Jens Ronneberger.

The "Lucky Moose" in Chinatown West is decorated with gold coins, the symbol for yin and yang, and the Chinese word for luck, written upside down to signify that good fortune has already arrived.

the sale of the moose statues after the event generated revenue for Canada's Olympic athletes and for local charities.

• • •

Chinatown East

By the 1970s a third Chinatown had emerged, this one located in the east end of Toronto, centred on Broadview Avenue and Gerrard Street. Newcomers from Hong Kong moved into this neighbourhood, which was already well-established, with schools, churches, and parks. Homes and business properties here were less expensive there than those in Old Chinatown and Chinatown West.

The first Chinese business was a meat store that was owned by Charlie Cheung.

Charlie's Meat and Seafood Store was the first Chinese business in Chinatown East.

Cheung arrived in 1952 from China when he was only twenty-three-years old. His first job was at Fat Laundry where he earned ten dollars a week. He slept at the back of the laundry because he couldn't afford a place of his own. Things looked up for him when he landed a job at Nanking Restaurant in Chinatown.

After working there for eighteen years, washing floors, cooking, and making deliveries, he saved up enough money and brought his wife to Canada. They bought a house on Beverley Street, close to Nanking Restaurant and to the business where she worked as a seamstress. When they both came home from work, they made cured meat, like Chinese

Lou Manning.

The Zhong Hua Men, or Chinese Arch, was erected in Chinatown East in 2009. It was recognized with the Award of Excellence by the International Parking Institute in 2012.

sausage, and sold it as a side business. Soon they had lots of restaurants that wanted to buy their meats. In 1971 they opened a store at 383A Broadview Avenue and called it Charlie's Meats. Following their lead other businesses opened and nearby homes were purchased or rented by the Chinese. Within a few years, there were four thousand Chinese living in Chinatown East.

Chinatown East has changed since those early years. New immigrants from Hong Kong invested heavily in the 1980s. Later a sizeable

Vietnamese population moved into the neighbourhood, creating a small community that was soon nicknamed "Little Saigon." More recently, new immigrants from mainland China have invested in the stores and restaurants there.

As more and more Chinese immigrants have come to Canada, they have increasingly looked for homes located not in the traditional Chinatowns but in Toronto's newer neighbourhoods.

• • •

Ethnoburbs

After the war soldiers returning home needed a place to live. Then, there was a baby boom, that is, a higher than normal number of babies were born into the families of these same veterans. Thousands of immigrants had also arrived from war-torn Europe. With these dramatic increases in the population, the demand for housing skyrocketed, but there weren't enough homes in Toronto. There was such a shortage that the city paid for newspaper ads warning, "Do not come to Toronto, Ontario, for housing accommodation."

Toronto was part of Metropolitan Toronto along with five suburbs: Etobicoke, York, North York, East York, and Scarborough.

The suburbs provided a solution to the housing shortage. There, new homes with large driveways and garages sprang up in quiet, safe, and new neighbourhoods on what was once farmland. These were being built, not house-by-house, but, rather, on a much larger scale, subdivision by subdivision, each one containing hundreds of homes.

A big factor that made suburban homes more appealing was the automobile, and people were buying cars like never before. The network of highways rapidly expanded to make driving more convenient. Shopping malls and office buildings with lots of parking space started appearing around major street intersections and highways.

With the explosion of the population in Metropolitan Toronto, there was talk about merging or amalgamating all of the city governments into one unified "megacity" — the new City of Toronto. Although this proposed merger was unpopular with most Torontonians, the megacity was established in 1998. Toronto, Etobicoke, York, North York, East York, and Scarborough merged into the new City of Toronto. Now there is one library system, one fire department, one police force, one public school board, one separate school board, one parks department, and so on.

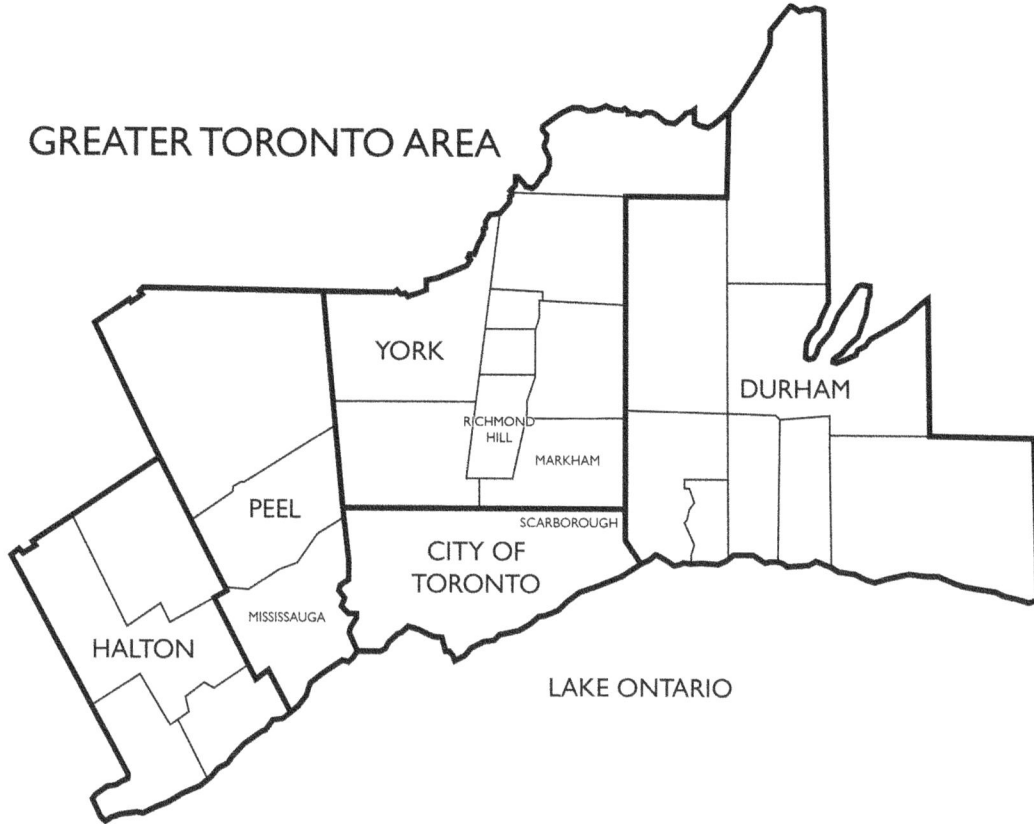

GREATER TORONTO AREA

YORK

RICHMOND
HILL

MARKHAM

DURHAM

PEEL

SCARBOROUGH

CITY OF
TORONTO

MISSISSAUGA

HALTON

LAKE ONTARIO

Michael Chan.

Large concentrations of Chinese are located in the City of Toronto (including Scarborough), and the neighbouring cities of Mississauga, Markham, and Richmond Hill.

This idea that "bigger is better" has inspired politicians and planners to think of something even bigger: the Greater Toronto Area (GTA). In addition to the new City of Toronto, the GTA includes the regions of York, Halton, Peel, and Durham. This entity, Canada's largest metropolitan area, has a population of over six million people.

During this time of government changes in Toronto, the traditional Chinatowns — Old Chinatown, Chinatown West, and Chinatown East — continued to be popular for shopping, eating, and the celebration of weddings, anniversaries, and Chinese festivals. However, the trend of moving away from downtown Toronto influenced the patterns of Chinese settlement. There wasn't much space left for all the newcomers coming into the city from Hong Kong, Taiwan, and China. As well, real estate prices for these downtown homes and businesses were soaring sky high.

• • •

Agincourt (Scarborough)

The Chinese in Toronto joined the move to the suburbs of Toronto. For them it was a dream come true: they could have a large house, big backyard, two-car garage, and lots of open space.

It became a mark of status to leave behind the older homes of the downtown neighbourhoods. This trend also showed how times had changed. Chinese Canadians no longer had to live in the traditional Chinatowns in downtown Toronto. They now had the option of living in the suburbs and their top choice was Scarborough. From 1971 and 2006, the population of Chinese people there increased dramatically.

TABLE 3: Chinese Population in Scarborough

1971	1,810
1986	30,120
1991	65,825
2006	117,405

Source: Census Canada.

What prompted the Chinese exodus out of downtown Toronto in 1984 was Dragon Centre, the first Chinese-themed mall in North America. Located in a neighbourhood called Agincourt, within the suburb of Scarborough, the mall opened with restaurants and stores catering specifically to Chinese customers. Unlike the Chinatowns in downtown Toronto, there were no streets and sidewalks filled with stores and restaurants. Instead, Dragon Centre was designed as an indoor mall with lots of parking space for suburban drivers and their cars.

An unexpected reaction from the Agincourt community exploded after this mall became popular. A parking shortage caused a spillover of automobiles onto the neighbouring streets, and local Scarborough residents complained loudly about the traffic problems, with some circulating racist, anti-Chinese flyers.

Despite the protests Dragon Centre was such a success that more Chinese-themed malls sprang up in Scarborough and other suburbs, like North York. These have been called, by some, Chinatowns. Many argue that these clusters of Chinese residents and businesses around malls should not really be called Chinatowns because they are so unlike the traditional ones in downtown Toronto. The term *ethnoburb* is arguably a more suitable label for these suburban Chinese communities that are appearing across North America.

This term was first used to more accurately describe the suburban neighbourhoods new Chinese residents in Los Angeles were settling into — neighbourhoods that were so different from the traditional Chinatowns the early immigrants had lived in. The differences between Chinatowns and ethnoburbs are significant: downtown vs. suburban, occu-

The Dragon Centre started the trend of Chinese-themed malls in Scarborough, Markham, Mississauga, and Richmond Hill.

pied by the working-class vs. skilled workers, lower vs. higher income residents, older vs. more recent immigrants, and accessible by public transport vs. car-friendly.

• • •

Mississauga

The Chinese malls in Toronto's suburbs were not the only ones that were attracting people away from the downtown Chinatowns. To the west of Toronto is the city of Mississauga. In 1961 there were only one hundred residents of Chinese heritage, a very small proportion of Mississauga's population of sixty-two thousand. The increases in the Chinese population there were gradual and the greatest numbers began arriving from 1981 onwards.

A group of Chinese businesses opened around the intersection of Dundas and Hurontario streets; however, a Chinese-themed mall that opened in 1988 became the big draw. A crew of sixty workers were brought from China to build replicas of famous historical sites, including the Nine Dragon Wall and the Great Wall of China. In 1998 the Mississauga Chinese Centre, whose address on Dundas Street is the lucky number 888, was recognized by Ontario as the first official tourist attraction in Mississauga.

Did You Know?

The Chinese believe in lucky numbers. The number eight is one example that is used to bring good fortune. In Cantonese this number is pronounced *bat* which rhymes with the word *fat*, meaning wealth and good luck. That is why so many car licence plates for Chinese drivers include this number. Even addresses for homes and businesses, as well as cell phones, have this number, if possible.

There are also unlucky numbers. The number four in Cantonese is pronounced *say*, which sounds like the word for death. Having this number on car licences or in home or business addresses is thought to bring bad luck. Many houses that are in popular neighbourhoods for Chinese residents have tried, with some success, to have their address numbers changed so that it doesn't have the number four.

Ruth Lor Malloy.

The Nine Dragon Wall features a dragon, the symbol of the emperor, surrounded by eight other flying dragons, all nine bringing good fortune.

The 2006 census reports that there are 46,125 Chinese in Mississauga, 7 percent of the city's population of 665,655. Unlike in Scarborough and downtown Toronto, the Chinese there live all over the city, rather than in clustered communities.

• • •

Richmond Hill and Markham

Richmond Hill and Markham are municipalities located on the northern edge of Toronto. Both are among the top Canadian cities to attract newcomers, especially those from Hong

Kong and China. The largest visible minority group in these communities is Chinese, with a population of 34,615 in Richmond Hill and 89,300 in Markham.[3] After English, Chinese is the most spoken language.

Profile

Ella Hung arrived in Toronto from China in 1980 with her husband, two children, and one hundred dollars. Their story shows the migration pattern from the city to the suburbs. They first lived in a basement apartment in downtown Toronto. Although they were both engineers, their living was made from repairing televisions and VCRs. After years of hard work, they saved and bought a home near Agincourt, then in Markham. In her words, "We are very lucky to be in Canada. It is heaven here."[4]

As Chinese immigrants flocked in, Asian-themed malls were built at a fast rate. Market Village, the first Chinese mall in Markham, opened in 1990; it was made up of small outdoor retail stores, in tribute to the old village roots of Markham. Next to Market Village is the Pacific Mall, which opened in 1996 as North America's largest Chinese indoor mall. Its construction was met with much resentment from the long-time residents in the neighborhood. They complained that the Chinese were taking over and driving away the "backbone of Markham." The Chinese community rallied to protest the racist reactions against Chinese Canadians.

Today the Pacific Mall is jam-packed with stores and shops that give shoppers the experience of shopping in Hong Kong or Beijing. Open year-round, even on Christmas Day, the fashion boutiques display traditional Chinese and modern Western clothes. Herbalists and teashops are set up alongside electronics stores and tailors' shops. The food court has a variety of Chinese cuisine. On the second floor, a replica of a colourful Chinese village market is crowded with shoppers, players at the arcade, and diners at the restaurants. Within three years of the opening of Pacific Mall, there were no less than fifty-eight Asian-themed malls in Scarborough, Markham, and Richmond Hill.

Pacific Mall.

The Pacific Mall is one of the most expensive and sought after addresses for Chinese businesses in the Greater Toronto Area.

• • •

The Need Was Great

Not only are these mega-malls populating the Greater Toronto Area, other developments of a different nature have been built. The Mon Sheong Home for the Aged, the first Chinese healthcare facility in Ontario, was opened at 36 Darcy Street in Chinatown West. This was in 1975, when health and housing care was sorely needed, especially for the aging men of the bachelor society. The early Chinese in Toronto were now seniors, many of whom lived in rundown rooming houses where they rented a single room and shared washroom and kitchen facilities with other boarders. Older women who had arrived to join their husbands after the repeal of the Exclusion Act were now widowed.

The need was great and a group of Chinese Canadians established the Mon Sheong Foundation, the first Chinese organization to obtain charitable status in Ontario. Money was raised to build a home to care for elderly Chinese. Since then the Mon Sheong Foundation has expanded the original building on Darcy Street, as well as added two nursing homes in Richmond Hill and Scarborough.

In 1994 the Yee Hong Centre for Geriatric Care opened at McNicoll and Midland avenues. Today Yee Hong has four centres in Scarborough, Markham, and Mississauga to provide care, housing, and medical services. They serve not only Chinese people but also others of diverse ethnic backgrounds.

The Mon Sheong Home for the Aged at 36 Darcy Street near Chinatown West was the first seniors housing project built for Chinese Canadians in Canada. Two additional locations have opened in Scarborough and Richmond Hill.

The Yee Hong Foundation raises 2.5 million dollars annually to support the four Yee Hong Centres for seniors in Scarborough, Markham, and Mississauga.

EIGHT

A Diverse Community

Although there are no more anti-Chinese laws, like the Chinese Exclusion Act, racist attitudes and perceptions still persist. When the Indochinese boat people came to Canada in the late 1970s, many Canadians expressed their objections over the high number of refugees. In the 1980s the newspapers sensationalized stories about the wealthy Chinese who were purchasing homes and businesses and reportedly driving up real estate prices.

A task force made up of representatives from key Chinese community organizations reported in 1977 that the Canadian view of the Chinese in Canada still perpetuated stereotyping "of the crudest order." The adjectives that were used to describe the Chinese included "sly, exotic, brutal, evil"; many believed that Chinese were not "normal human beings." According to the task force findings, the occupations that were perceived as typical for Chinese were "waiters, houseboys, prostitutes, villains, cooks, gardeners and fiery kung fu experts."[1] All of this was shocking; however, it was a short, eleven-minute television documentary, "Campus Giveaway," that mobilized the Chinese community to stage a nation-wide protest on a scale never before seen.

• • •

Campus Giveaway

In 1979 *W5*, a CTV program, aired a segment titled "Campus Giveaway." It portrayed Chinese students as foreigners who were taking away spaces from Canadian students in professional schools such as law and medicine. It started with this opening voice-over: "Suppose your son or daughter wanted to be an engineer, or a doctor, or a pharmacist.

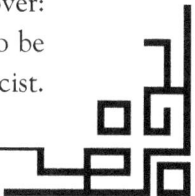

Suppose he had high marks in high school, and that you could pay the tuition — but he still couldn't get into university in his chosen courses because a foreign student was taking his place. Well, that is exactly what is happening in the country."[2]

Protests came from students and supporters across Canada who demanded an apology for irresponsible journalism. Not only were there many factual errors in the television program, but it portrayed Chinese Canadians in a negative way and labelled the Asian students as "foreigners." In fact the Chinese faces belonged to Canadian citizens. With a collective voice never before seen, Toronto's Chinese community staged protest activities, which included the largest march ever in Chinese-Canadian history. Eventually, the CTV network apologized and admitted that its program had "distorted the actual statistics" and that "the majority of the research data was incorrect."

Another outcome was the formation of the Chinese Canadian National Council, an organization to fight for equality on behalf of the Chinese community. The council and its local chapters across Canada have worked tirelessly on issues that challenge Chinese Canadians. In 2005 the Toronto chapter was the recipient of the City of Toronto's William P. Hubbard Award for Race Relations.

• • •

Head Tax Campaign

In 1984 a man named Dak Leon Mark visited his member of Parliament in Vancouver. His purpose was simple. He wanted a refund from the government for the five hundred dollar head tax that he had paid when he came to Canada. His request was turned down; however, what happened next made history.

For the next twenty-two years, four thousand head tax payers and their families, as well as thousands of supporters across Canada, demanded financial compensation for the discriminatory head tax. Between 1885 and 1923, eighty thousand Chinese immigrants had collectively paid twenty-three million dollars in head taxes, a sum valued today at 1.2 billion dollars.

Six prime ministers later, Prime Minister Stephen Harper apologized to the head tax payers, their families, and the Chinese-Canadian community. In 2006 he stated: "On behalf of all Canadians and the Government of Canada, we offer a full apology to Chinese Canadians for the head tax and express our deepest sorrow for the subsequent exclusion of Chinese immigrants."[3]

Compensation was paid to head tax survivors, which at the time numbered only forty, and to the widows of deceased head tax payers. In addition over thirty million dollars was allocated for projects to recognize the contributions of the Chinese community in Canada. Dak Leon Mark did not live to see the successful outcome of his request for a refund.

• • •

A Painful Choice

Although many of the terrible things Chinese immigrants had to deal with in the past are now gone, today's immigrants still face difficulties — and difficult choices. With all of the Chinese immigrants coming to Canada from Hong Kong, Taiwan, and China, a new family arrangement has developed, especially since the 1980s. Business people and entrepreneurs have come to Canada in large numbers, believing it a safer and more secure country for their families. Although they bring experience and skills developed in Asia, it hasn't always been as easy as they thought it would be to replicate their business successes in Canada. Many have found that different circumstances, including higher taxes and stricter laws, make it more challenging for them to make as much money in Canada as they can at home. As a result many continue to conduct their businesses in Asia. Although their families have settled in Canada, they remain in their original homes. They have become known as "astronauts," because they are constantly flying back and forth across the Pacific Ocean. An estimated one-quarter of Chinese-Canadian families in the Greater Toronto Area have an astronaut in their family.[4]

Sometimes the parents stay in Canada while their children are raised in Asia by their grandparents or other relatives. One Toronto woman made the painful choice of sending her five-year-old daughter and seven-month-old son to China because she didn't have any family or friends to look after her children. "It's too expensive to put two kids in daycare. I don't have any support," she says.[5] In the Greater Toronto Area, an estimated two thousand Canadian-born Chinese are sent to mainland China each year, then returned to Canada when they are old enough to start kindergarten.

Many children of wealthy families come to Canada as students because of the tough competition to get into prestigious schools, universities, and colleges in Asia. Imagine travelling to a new country as a teenager to start high school, university, or college while parents, families, and friends are thousands of miles away. These overseas students have to learn how to live on their own and deal with matters that normally are looked after by their parents.

• • •

Adopted Daughters

While life can be difficult for children whose parents are far away, it is even more difficult for those without parents or families. China has many such children. In 1989 China opened their orphanages for adoption to families from around the world. These orphanages were full of children, especially baby girls, waiting for someone to adopt them. Why were there so many? The reason is China's one-child policy. By tradition Chinese have a preference for sons rather than daughters, because sons carry on the family name and take on the role of the head of the family. If a couple starts a family and a daughter is born, the baby girl is often abandoned at an orphanage so that the couple has a second chance to have a boy.

From 2000 to 2007, over six thousand children were adopted by Canadian families, mostly from Ontario and Quebec.[6] There are organizations that help families with adopted children. In Toronto the organization Families with Children from China has over 350 member families. The Friendship Program at the Chinese Cultural Centre of Greater Toronto brings together families with adopted children and immigrants from China so that adopted children have a chance to learn about their culture and heritage.

• • •

Where Are You Really From?

The question of identity is another difficult issue for many Chinese Canadians. Who are Chinese Canadians? Many are among the influx of Chinese immigrants who have come to Canada recently; there are many others who can trace their family arrivals back several generations. Some come from Hong Kong, some from Taiwan. Today there are a great many new profiles of Chinese Canadians, depending on when their family members arrived or were born, from which country they arrived, and at what time period. Each family is different.

Emily Chou.

Where are you really from?

Chinese Canadians, born and raised in Canada, are a sizeable group and make up 25 percent of the Chinese population. They look Chinese and their parents may have very different backgrounds but they are Canadian in their outlook. "Canadian-born [Chinese] are like bananas: yellow on the outside and white inside.... We have so many white attitudes and values, but our skin is yellow," commented Fern Hum, who lives in Chinatown.[7]

Jean Lumb remembered, "We are Chinese, so we're visible. A European could blend into this society without much notice, but a Chinese is a Chinese."[8]

Fiona was born in Toronto in 1971. She remembers how isolated she felt attending high school. "I didn't want to be Chinese. I wanted to be white because all my friends were white.... When you're a teenager you want to be like everybody else and I looked different and my grandmother didn't speak English."[9]

Canadian-born Chinese, however, are far out-numbered by Chinese newcomers. Some are known as "the 1.5 generation"; this group is made up of young people who arrive in Canada before or during their early teens. They bring with them the culture of their home country and quickly pick up the traditions of Canadian life, a combination of the new and the old.

It isn't uncommon for Chinese Canadians to be told that they speak such good English or to be asked where they were born. For many, having a dual identity makes them question how they can live in two worlds. Some parents worry that their children are losing their Chinese culture if they do not speak the language or follow all of the traditions. Perhaps the changing identity of Canadian-born Chinese is a natural process in a multicultural country like Canada. As the father of Jean Lumb advised her, "Don't keep it all — only the better things from two worlds."[11] In the words of Gretta (Wong) Grant, "We should take the best from each society."[12]

Profile

"There was one time back in Grade 7 or Grade 8 that I kind of [felt] that I [was] Canadian and not Chinese, but I can't really hide that way because I do not know about the Canadian culture as much as my other white friends do.... In Grade 9 summer school I met a group of friends that I am with now and ever since then. They are all Chinese, and we find that we are very attached to each other and to the Chinese culture... I am not trying to hide the fact that I am so much Chinese and I know that I am not pure Canadian."[10]

• • •

Speaking, Reading, and Writing Chinese

One of the most important things for the Chinese, as with all people, is their language. The national language of China and Taiwan is Mandarin, which is the most spoken language around the globe. There are also hundreds of dialects of Chinese, each with different expressions, pronunciations, and vocabulary. Each province, town, and village has its own dialect, some so different that people cannot understand one another from province to province, and village to village. The language groupings include Yue (Cantonese and Taishanese), Wu (Shanghainese), Minnan (Hokkien-Taiwanese) and Hakka. That is why the national language of Mandarin is so important: it provides a common language for the many people who speak all of the diverse dialects. Today people in China speak Mandarin as well as their own local dialect.

The Chinese language, considered one of the world's oldest written languages, is made up of symbols called Chinese characters. Some characters represent objects, such as a table or tree. Others are formed by combining two or more characters, like the combination of sun and moon to make the word for bright. There are over fifty thousand characters in the written language, but knowledge of only two or three thousand is needed to read a newspaper.

Many Chinese words have the same sound as other words, but have different meanings, just as in English there are homonyms such as to, two, and too. Sometimes the same word can be spoken with different tones that change the meaning. Mandarin has four tones while Cantonese has nine. For example the word for mother and horse is *ma* but pronounced with different tones. You wouldn't want to call your mother a horse, would you?

As confusing as the language can be, the Chinese have great fun making puns, rhymes, and plays on words. One of the most famous people in China today is a Canadian hailing from Richmond Hill — Mark Rowswell, better known by millions of Chinese as DaShan (Big Mountain). His mastery of the Chinese language has made him a household name for his comedy performance that is rich in jokes, storytelling, teasing, and voice imitations.

• • •

Traditional or Simplified?

Although Chinese is very difficult to learn to read and write, it was easier when there was only one way to write Chinese. It didn't matter which dialect was spoken because the written Chinese was the same. Now, there are two writing styles — traditional and simplified Chinese (see Table 4).

TABLE 4: Traditional and Simplified Chinese

English	Traditional Chinese	Simplified Chinese	Pinyin
China	中國	中国	Zhongguo

Simplified Chinese was introduced by the Chinese government in the 1950s to help improve literacy. Many Chinese characters were simplified by reducing the number of strokes. For example there are two characters for China (see Table 4). The first character, *Zhong*, is the same in traditional and simple Chinese; however, the second character, *guo*, has fewer strokes in the simplified version than the traditional one.

Although simplified Chinese is the official writing system in China, traditional Chinese is still used in Hong Kong, Macau, Singapore, and Taiwan. The distinction can be seen in Chinese newspapers. Three major ones — *Sing Tao*, *Ming Pao*, and *World Journal* — use the traditional characters while the newspapers in China are published with simplified Chinese characters.

• • •

Ni Hao Ma?

For people who can't read or write Chinese, a new and modern system called "pinyin" was introduced to write Mandarin in English using the Latin alphabet. For example the question, "How are you," would be *Ni hao ma?* in pinyin. This system is widely used in China on street, airport, and road signs and as a way for teaching Chinese as a second language.

Because the pinyin system is only applied to Mandarin Chinese, and not to all of the other Chinese dialects, the English spelling of Chinese names can be very confusing. As an example, the surname *Wong* is spelled in the following ways, depending on the language or dialect being spoken (see Table 5).

Did You Know?

When the Communist government was established in 1949, China's literacy rate was 20 percent. That means that only one person in five could read and write. Teaching literacy was one of the country's top priorities as it sought to educate its workforce and modernize the economy. As a result the government simplified the written forms of many traditional characters in the 1950s to make reading and writing easier. It was decided that if a famer could read 1,500 characters and if an office worker or city resident could read two thousand characters then they would be considered literate. By those standards China's literacy rate today is more than 90 percent, a remarkable achievement in sixty years.

TABLE 5: Spelling the Surname Wong

Chinese Language or Dialect	English Spelling
Mandarin	Huang
Cantonese, Taishanese, Fukyianese, Hakka	Wone, Wong
Vietnamese	Huynh, Hoang
Fukien	Oei, Oi, Ooi, Uy, Wee
Hokkien, Teochew	Ng, Ong, Ung

Source: *Chuck W.C. Wong, The Wong Family Name (Wong's National Convention 2011), 1.*

Up until the 1960s, the Chinese dialect that was spoken in Toronto was Taishanese. This is the language of people who came from villages in the province of Guangdong. Most early immigrants were young, poor peasants who were illiterate. They had never learned to read or write because they couldn't afford an education and they were too busy working in the fields. The few who could read and write often earned their living writing and reading letters. It was not an uncommon sight to see a lineup of men waiting to have a letter written to their loved ones in China or to have a letter from China read to them.

The influx of Chinese immigrants from around the world has changed what is heard on the streets of Toronto. The arrival of large numbers of Cantonese speakers from Hong Kong has resulted in Taishanese becoming less common. Now, with the arrival of newcomers from China, Taiwan, and Singapore, Mandarin is becoming more prevalent. Other dialects, such as Hakka, Shanghainese, and Hokkien, can also be heard on the streets.

Today new immigrants are eager to have their children speak, read, and write Chinese. Due to the efforts of the Chinese community to establish language programs in the 1970s, Chinese, as well as other languages, are taught during regular classroom hours at some schools. Other Chinese-language classes are provided across the city. Chinese churches, like the Chinese Presbyterian Church, offered classes as early as 1919 and the Mon Sheong Foundation started providing them in 1970. Chinese-language courses are also widely offered at colleges, universities, and private schools.

• • •

Lucky Money and Moon Cakes

Language is an important part of Chinese culture, but there are many other important aspects. More and more, Chinese culture, traditions, and festivals, celebrated every year in Toronto, have become a part of Canadian life.

The most important festival in the Chinese calendar is *Chun Jie*, the Spring Festival, more commonly known as Chinese New Year. It lasts for fifteen days, starting on New Year's Eve. Many special foods such as *nian gao*, or New Year's cake, are shared with family and friends. Children look forward to this festival the most because they receive so much "lucky money" in small, red envelopes. The festivities are celebrated with dragon and lion dances, music, dance, opera performances, and other celebratory events. Chinese greet the Spring Festival with as much anticipation and enthusiasm as Christmas, Easter, Thanksgiving, and other Western holidays.

The Pure Brightness Festival, or *Qing Ming*, is a time to visit the cemetery and pay respect to deceased ancestors and family members. It is customary to burn incense and place food such as chicken and roast pork at the gravesites.

The Dragon Boat Festival, or *Duan Wu Jie*, falls on the fifth day of the fifth month. It is a day to remember the great Chinese poet and patriot Qu Yuan, whose drowning over two thousand years ago is commemorated with dragon boat races and the eating of sticky rice dumplings, or *zhongzi*. The Toronto Chinese Business Association started Toronto's first annual dragon boat race

Pauline Chong.

The youth chapter of the Chinese Cultural Centre of Greater Toronto in Scarborough promotes Chinese culture and develops leaders of tomorrow.

in 1989 with twenty-seven teams. Now in its twenty-fourth year, this event is attended by 180 teams and over five thousand Chinese and non-Chinese athletes. Dragon boating has spread across the Greater Toronto Area to other parts of Canada. Such races are held in over forty other countries also, and the

number is growing. It is now one of the fastest growing sports in the world.

The Mid-Autumn Festival, or *Zhong Qui Jie*, falls on the fifteenth day of the eighth month, when the moon is at its fullest and brightest in the year. Families gather to share moon cakes and feast on a sumptuous meal together. The largest moon cake ever made was created in Chinatown West in 2001. Measuring 4.41 metres long and 2.74 metres wide and weighing 2.28 tonnes, it earned a spot in the *Guinness Book of World Records.*

The last major festival of the year, Winter Solstice Festival, or *Dong Zhi*, is an occasion for families to give thanks for the past year and to thank the kitchen god so he will bring prosperity in the new year. A sweet soup made of little rice dumplings is shared as a symbol of family togetherness and good luck.

Chinese culture and traditions, such as these, are fostered across the Greater Toronto Area and particularly at the Chinese Cultural Centre of Greater Toronto, the largest of its kind in North America. At the entrance are two majestic lions that welcome visitors who come to share Chinese heritage, learn to speak Chinese, and participate in cultural activities such as crafts, cooking, art, and music.

• • •

Martial Arts

Probably one of the most well-known aspects of Chinese culture is its tradition of martial arts. Martial arts, or kung fu, have been practised for thousands of years in China. Before World War Two, Chinatown was the only place to learn martial arts, but in those days enrolment was restricted to Chinese students only. This changed in the early 1960s when Jimmy Lore opened the Jing Mo Kung Fu Club on Hagerman Street in Chinatown. Nicknamed Demon Fighter, he was the first Canadian martial arts teacher to teach kung fu to non-Chinese students. Lore was the *sifu*, or teacher, of the two-time world figure skating champion and Olympic silver-medalist Elvis Stojko, who incorporated many kung fu movements into his routine and skated to the theme music of *Little Dragon*, the 1982 movie about Bruce Lee.

Another martial arts pioneer was Paul Chan, who established the Hong Luck Kung Fu Club in 1961. It was another one of the early martial arts training centres and schools to teach non-Chinese students in Canada.

By the 1970s action movies and the fast moves of Bruce Lee, as Kato in *The Green Hornet* television series and in his numerous kung fu films, made martial arts popular in North America. Today clubs and schools such as the Sunny Tang Martial Arts Centre, which now has more than ten locations in Canada, provide classes for students, both Chinese and non-Chinese. Through intense

Ian Chow.

Students of Southern Legs, Northern Fists train in close-range sparring, which tests their martial arts skills.

training using traditional forms and styles, such as Wing Chun and Shaolin, students learn punches, kicks, blocks, and strikes to defend themselves, as well as improve their concentration and mental strength.

Kung fu clubs perform at store openings, wedding parties, and community events. More often than not, a lively lion dance is the showcase for the skills of the participants. The lion dance has two performers, one for the

A lion dance is performed in the 1960s.

Jean Lamb Collection.

large, colourful head with its blinking eyes and shaggy beard, one for the long tail. They walk, strut, kick, and leap, to the delight of the audience. The lion brings good luck through its intricate and lively movements. For very special occasions, the dragon dance is performed. A majestic dragon head is carried on a long pole and its long, serpent-like tail is manipulated by at least nine people to mimic the gracefully flowing motion of the dragon.

A gentler form of martial art is tai chi, often practised outdoors in parks and open spaces. This involves a graceful and slow-moving sequence of movements, similar in many ways to yoga and meditation; the movements are designed to help *qi*, or vital energy, to move around the body.

• • •

Dishes, Familiar and New

Even more than martial arts, though, Chinese food is the best known part of Chinese culture. Many Canadians first learn about Chinese culture by eating at a Chinese restaurant. They try to use chopsticks. They'll hear Chinese being spoken — Mandarin, Cantonese, or some other dialect. They point to steaming items that are offered from *dim sum* carts. These could be crescent-shaped dumplings filled with shrimp, spareribs in a black bean sauce, or sesame-covered balls with lotus seed. Dishes, familiar and new, can be ordered from the menu or from the specials posted on the wall.

Chinese restaurants can be found in Chinatown and all across the Greater Toronto Area. Some are large and noisy with seating for up to a thousand diners. Others are smaller, family-run eateries with simple menus. Many restaurants specialize in certain types of food — noodles, congee (rice soup), bubble tea, Taiwanese cuisine, spicy Sichuan food, and so on. Diners who might prefer more variety can visit buffets with over one hundred Chinese and Western dishes. Home delivery and take out are fast, convenient options for busy families.

Did You Know?

Where did the English word *chopstick* comes from? It has its origin in pidgin, a mixture of Chinese and English. Trade between Britain and China began in the 1600s, and to help with communication, pidgin was developed. In Chinese pidgin "chop" meant "quick" — "chop chop" is still in use today to mean "hurry." The Chinese word for chopsticks means "quick sticks"; that became "chopsticks" in the English language.[13]

At home people cook the Chinese way without a second thought. They stir-fry fresh vegetables and meat in a *wok* (Chinese frying pan) and add Chinese spices and sauces such as ginger, garlic, and soy sauce. Bamboo steamers and rice cookers are stored in kitchen cupboards with the pots and pans. Chopsticks are in the silverware drawer alongside forks, knives, and spoons.

For ingredients, shoppers make their way through the streets of Chinatown. Crates and boxes spill over with vegetables like bok choy, and exotic fruits such as dragon fruit and the spiky, smelly durian. Dried foods include soybean curd, mushrooms, and seafood such as fish and shrimp. Noodles of all sorts, made of rice flour or wheat, are offered alongside bags of rice — short-grain, long-grain, glutinous, and fragrant. Live fish, lobsters, crabs, clams, and mussels wait to be picked out of their holding tanks. Whole roasted ducks and chickens hang in the barbecue store windows. Even local grocery stores such as Metro and Loblaws supply Chinese ingredients because of the high demand from their customers.

As Canada has come to embrace diversity more and more, Chinese food and culture have carved out an increasingly important spot in Canadian life. There's no doubt that credit for the acceptance of this treasure trove of cultural traditions and experiences is due to the efforts of outstanding individuals from the Chinese-Canadian community.

NINE

Noted Toronto Chinese

Many Chinese Canadians have distinguished themselves in a variety of fields. The early Chinese were trailblazers in their own right, quietly but steadfastly facing daily discrimination. Although their life stories may not seem that remarkable or ground-breaking, their success in their lives were small miracles, given the historical context of those early years. There's an old saying: "The journey is as important as the destination." Thousands are nameless in the history books but so much is owed to their courage and determination, the results of which are so evident today.

• • •

Science and Technology

Consider the scientific advances by Toronto Chinese, four of whom have been honoured with the Order of Canada:

- The discovery of the gene responsible for cystic fibrosis in 1989 has been attributed to the work of distinguished geneticist Lap Chee Tsui (1950–).
- Tak Wah Mak (1946–) is internationally recognized as one of Canada's most accomplished research scientists. His co-discovery of the T-cell receptor accelerated advances in immunology, molecular biology, and the understanding of diseases such as multiple sclerosis and cancer;
- Kue Young (1948–) is a leader in health research and the delivery of health services to Canada's First Nations peoples living in remote communities;
- Neville Poy, who is a retired plastic surgeon and an avid photographer, holds the rank of honorary colonel of the Queen's York Rangers Regiment of the army's reserve forces — the first Chinese-

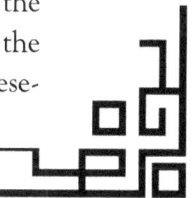

Canadian colonel. He was named to the Order of Canada for his ground-breaking medical achievements.

Younger Chinese Canadians have also begun to make their mark in science. Recently, a sixteen-year-old high school student from Richmond Hill made a discovery that could help the fight against cystic fibrosis. After doing computer simulations at the Hospital for Sick Children's Research Institute, Marshall Zhang tested a theory; the results show great promise.

His work at the hospital was not obtained without persistence and perseverance, qualities common in the spirit of the early Chinese immigrants in Canada. To his credit, he landed a spot in the Hospital for Sick Children's research lab after searching long and hard for a scientist who would work with him. "Most of them said 'no' because I didn't have the experience I needed," he said. "I emailed the entire list of faculty in biochemistry at the University of Toronto. The last one said yes."[1]

Two Toronto teenagers from Agincourt Collegiate were catapulted into the headlines when they sent a Lego man into the stratosphere in 2012. Mathew Ho and Asad Muhammad, with little budget but endless ingenuity, captured on film their Lego man flying high in the air, carrying a Canadian flag against a backdrop of endless space.

• • •

Sports

Chinese Canadians have also made their mark in sports. When most people in Canada think of sports played on the ice, they don't usually think of figure skating. Yet, this sport has put the country in the forefront for gold-medal wins. Twenty-one-year-old figure skater Patrick Chan, who graduated from École secondaire Étienne-Brûlé in North York, has captured the hearts of Canadians as the six-time Canadian champion, two-time world champion, and the recipient of the 2011 Lou Marsh Award for Canada's top athlete.

Markham's Michelle Li is Canada's top-rated singles and doubles badminton player and is a two-time Pan Am champion. A student at the University of Toronto, she took a two-year break to concentrate on representing Canada at the London Olympics in 2012. She finished in fourth place in the doubles event.

Gerard Chataigneau.

Patrick Chan skates to first place at the 2011 Canadian Figure Skating Championships in Victoria, British Columbia, after landing two quad jumps.

Christine Lee, better known to her fans as Peng Peng, has been a competitive contender and award-winner in Canadian gymnastics. Born in Scarborough she was Canada's top performer at the 2011 world championship and the top Canadian in the Olympic qualifying competition. A few months before the Olympics, an injury forced her withdrawal; however, she travelled to London as the honorary captain of the women's gymnastics team.

• • •

Literature

Chinese-Canadian actors, musicians, and writers are well known across the country and around the world. A number of writers have created distinctive voices that capture the Canadian sense of place, whether that place is a city or a small town, and the essence of Chinese identity. Award-winning children's author Paul Yee, who moved to Toronto from Vancouver, has written twenty-eight books of poetry, short stories, novels, and history, including *Tales of Gold Mountain*, *Ghost Train*, and *Saltwater City*.

Judy Fong Bates, who was born in China, came to Canada as a young girl. She grew up in small-town Ontario and moved to Toronto as an adult to work as an elementary school teacher. Her works, which include the novel *Midnight at the Dragon Cafe*, the short-story collection *China Dogs and Other Stories*, and the family memoir *The Year of Finding Memory* are award-winning and critically acclaimed.

Jan Wong, who was born in Montreal, is an award-winning journalist and author who has written extensively about China and her experience living there. She divides her time between Toronto, where she writes for *Toronto Life* magazine, and New Brunswick, where she teaches at St. Thomas University and writes for the *Halifax Chronicle Herald*.

Vincent Lam, who was born in London, Ontario, juggles two professions, working as an emergency room doctor in Toronto

Author Paul Yee with Baxter.

and as a writer. His first book, *Bloodletting and Miraculous Cures*, won the prestigious Scotiabank Giller Prize in 2006. Lam's first novel, *The Headmaster's Wager*, was short-listed for the Governor General's Award.

Wayson Choy is an award-winning novelist, memoirist, and short-story writer who grew up in Vancouver before his move to Toronto. Among his works are *The Jade Peony*, *Paper Shadows*, and *All that Matters*. Each of these works provides moving and illuminating stories about the history of the Chinese community. He received the Order of Canada in 2005.

• • •

Music

Chinese Canadians have enriched the music scene in Canada with their performances and compositions.

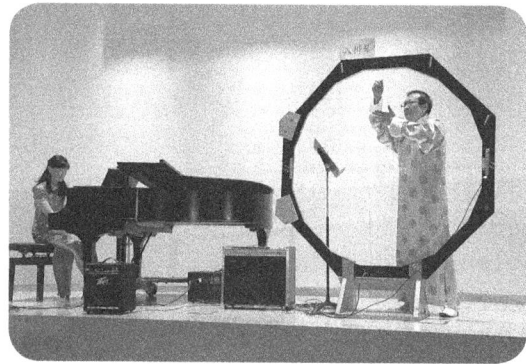

Chan Ka Nin on Ba Gua Qin stringed instrument and Alice Ho on piano.

- Alexina Louie, who is an accomplished classical musician and composer for orchestras, symphonies, dance, film, and television, explores and expresses her Chinese roots through her award-winning music.
- Chan Ka Nin is a composer who has won many awards, including two Junos for his musical compositions that draw from both Eastern and Western influences. His opera *Iron Road*, set during the construction of the Canadian Pacific Railway, was adapted into a feature film starring Tony Leung, Peter O'Toole, and Sam Neil.
- Alice Ping Yee Ho is an acclaimed solo pianist and composer who has received many national and international awards for her works, which are inspired by Chinese folk music and opera, Japanese taiko and African drumming, and jazz.
- Sook-Yin Lee is the host of the CBC Radio's *Definitely Not the Opera*. Her varied career includes MuchMusic VJ, lead singer in the bands Bob's Your Uncle and Slan, solo artist, filmmaker, and actor in theatre, film, and television.
- Donald Quan is a musician, and film and television composer for shows such as *Mutant X* and *Relic Hunter*. His Toronto store, Musideum, is the first and only one in Canada that sells musical instruments from around the world.

• • •

Film and Theatre

The representation of actors of Chinese heritage in Canadian film, theatre, and television has been gradually increasing. Works produced by Fu-GEN Asian Canadian Theatre Company have provided opportunities to present Asian-Canadian talent, while others have found roles in mainstream film and theatre.

Judy Jiao played the character of Leia Chang on the television show *Degrassi: The Next Generation*. Her parents emigrated from China to Toronto, where her mother was an engineering professor at the University of Toronto. Although she recognized that acting was an unlikely career path, she pursued acting with her parents' blessings. "To be doing something in the entertainment industry is definitely non-traditional." Jiao, who left acting, is currently studying business at Harvard University.[2]

Scarborough-born Ellen Wong attended L'Amoreaux Collegiate, then went on to Ryerson University to major in film and television. "When I went to see *Titanic* with my parents as a girl, I was so moved by Kate Winslet's performance, and Leonardo DiCaprio. She inspired me to be an actress. That was the moment that I knew what I wanted to do. That's kind of how it all got started."[3] Among her acting roles are Knives Chau in *Scott Pilgrim vs. The World* and Nurse Suzy Chao in *Combat Hospital*. She has also received an ACTRA nomination for her role in *Silent Cargo* as an illegal immigrant who was smuggled across the ocean in a shipping container.

Actor Keanu Reeves, a Canadian of Chinese descent, grew up in Toronto where he attended Jesse Ketchum Public School, then four high schools, including Etobicoke School of the Arts, North Toronto Collegiate, and De La Salle Oaklands College. He has acted in over fifty films, including *Bill & Ted's Bogus Journey*, *The Matrix* trilogy, and *Speed*.

Filmmakers are uncovering stories of Chinese-Canadian history, and Keith Lock was one of the first filmmakers to do so. A graduate of York University, he has produced many celebrated works, and has been recognized with a Gemini Award nomination, a National Film Board award, and many other accolades.

• • •

Political Participation

The Chinese in Canada have a long history of political activism. In the early years, their focus was on political changes happening in China. During the head tax and exclusionary period, they had little to do with Canada's politics because they were denied the vote, discouraged from becoming citizens, and discriminated against by racist laws.

Since the end of World War Two, political activism has developed significantly, with Chinese Canadians taking interest in righting the wrongs of the past — misrepresentation of the W5 television program, recognition of the contribution of the CPR workers, and apology and compensation for the head tax. Other issues have rallied the Chinese community and produced many outstanding leaders.

Already mentioned is Jean Lumb, who led the Save Chinatown Committee to fight against the further destruction of Old Chinatown. Tam Goosen, a former school trustee and president of the Urban Alliance on Race Relation, has worked with many immigrant and visible minority groups. Dora Nipp, who is an author and filmmaker, is at the forefront on human rights matters affecting Chinese Canadians. Lawyer Avvy Go works in legal clinics to help low-income people, especially immigrants and refugees. A recipient of the City of Toronto's William P. Hubbard Award for Race Relations, she has been active in the Chinese Canadian National Council and Urban Alliance on Race Relation, as well as the co-founder of Colour of Poverty Campaign.

Winnie Ng is a worker rights activist who has been the recipient of many distinctions, including the Urban Alliance on Race Relations' Leadership Award, the United Farm Workers' Cesar Chavez Black Eagle Award, and the YWCA Woman of Distinction Award. Her late husband, Eugene Yao, fought for the rights of garment workers. He helped establish English-language classes for them and later served as the president of the Chinese Canadian National Council.

Joseph Y.K. Wong, whose humanitarian causes include the United Way and Save Elizabeth Lue Campaign, is an influential community leader and advocate of human rights, race relations, multiculturalism, and national unity. He is the founder of Yee Hong Centre for Geriatric Care, founding president of the Chinese Canadian National Council, and spokesperson for the Chinese Head Tax Redress Campaign.

Cheuk Kwan is a community activist and leader who has fought for equality for Chinese Canadians, such as the protest against the W5 television program. He helped to establish the Chinese Canadian National Council, an Asian-Canadian magazine, and the Harmony Movement. He is the director and producer of a thirteen-episode documentary, *Chinese Restaurants*.

Representation of Chinese Canadians in the political arena has been slowly increasing.

Up until 1947 many discriminatory obstacles prevented Chinese Canadians from getting involved in politics or the justice system. It was Douglas Jung who broke the barrier when he was elected in Vancouver as the first Chinese Canadian in the federal Parliament. Since then others have joined in the fight for people's rights as lawyers, judges, politicians, and government officials.

K. Dock Yip was born in Vancouver in 1906, as the seventeenth of twenty-four children born to Yip Sang, one of the city's most prominent men. Since Chinese were not permitted to study and practise law in British Columbia, Dock Yip moved to Toronto to enrol at the Osgoode Hall Law School, where he graduated in 1945 as Canada's first Chinese-Canadian lawyer. He opened a law office in Toronto's Chinatown at 117A Elizabeth Street. One year later, Gretta (Wong) Grant graduated from the same law school as the first woman of Chinese descent in Canada to become a lawyer.

Adrienne Clarkson was the first Asian Canadian appointed as Governor General of Canada. Born in Hong Kong, she came to Canada as a young child. "We arrived with one suitcase apiece and nothing else.... We still faced numerous uncertainties. One ... was that Canada at that point didn't welcome or particularly want non-white immigrants or refugees who were not white."[4] Clarkson became one of Canada's best-known media personalities in television and journalism, and she had a rich career in writing and film-making. She also served as the first Agent General for Ontario in France and president of McClelland and Stewart. A public school in Richmond Hill is named in her honour.

Vivienne Poy, who came to Canada in 1959, has achieved success as a fashion designer, entrepreneur, author, academic, and philanthropist. Poy was appointed to the Senate of Canada as its first Canadian of Asian descent. When she was called, she was so surprised. "It was very unexpected ... like a bolt from the sky."[5] Her achievements as senator include the introduction of a motion that led to the establishment of May as Asian Heritage Month. Another accomplishment was her successful campaign to change the lyrics to Canada's national anthem. As a result of her efforts, the sexist line "in all our sons command" was changed to the more inclusive "in all of us command." Breaking another barrier, she was the first person of a visible minority to be appointed as the Chancellor of the University of Toronto.

Neville Poy.

Senator Vivienne Poy.

Beginning in the 1970s, many Chinese Canadians have been elected to serve at all three levels of government as a voice for their constituents, both Chinese and non-Chinese. Although Chinese Canadians are still under-represented, political participation is increasing, notably in the 2010 Toronto municipal elections when a record number of candidates were elected.

Currently, there are three Chinese-Canadian members of Parliament (MPs) from the Greater Toronto Area. At the federal level, MP Olivia Chow represents Trinity-Spadina, the riding for Chinatown West. Prior to her election as MP, she was the first Asian woman elected as a Toronto city councillor. In the provincial legislature, MPP Michael Chan, who represents Markham-Unionville, is serving as the Minister of Tourism, Culture, and Sport, and as Minister Responsible for the 2015 Pan/Parapan American Games. Soo Wong, a former school trustee, is the MPP for Scarborough-Agincourt.

In the Greater Toronto Area, city councillors of Chinese heritage include Denzil Minnan-Wong, Chin Lee, Kristyn Wong-Tam, Alan Ho, Willie Woo, Alex Chiu, Jim Kwan, Joe Li, Godwin Chan, Castro Liu, and Sandra Yeung. School trustees include Shaun Chen, Ada Yeung, Allan Tam, Carol Chan, Jean Wong-Chong, and Nicolas Ayuen.

• • •

Philanthropists

Generosity of spirit has been demonstrated by many Chinese Torontonians, too numerous to list, but there are some of particular distinction. Raymond Chang is a Canadian business leader and philanthropist who was named the chancellor of Ryerson University in 2006. The G. Raymond Chang School of Continuing Education is named in recognition of his generosity.

Michael Lee-Chin is a businessman who gives back to his community as an act of gratitude for the opportunities that he has had since his arrival from Jamaica as an immigrant. His generous donation to the Royal Ontario Museum has been acknowledged by the museum, which named its new addition the Michael Lee-Chin Crystal after its recent renovation.

• • •

Firsts

Other Chinese Canadians are known for breaking glass ceilings to be the first in their fields:

- Robert (Bob) Wong, a former math and physics teacher at Northview Heights Secondary School, became the first cabinet minister of Chinese descent in the Ontario government in 1987;
- Chan Han Goh was the first Asian ballet dancer in the National Ballet of Canada;
- Hsio Yen Shih, who was a former curator of the Royal Ontario Museum, was the first Chinese Canadian to serve as director of the National Gallery of Canada;
- Susan Eng was the first Chinese Canadian to chair the Metropolitan Toronto Police Services Board;
- Ying Hope became the first Chinese Canadian elected as a school trustee to the Toronto Board of Education in 1964; he was elected as chair in 1968;
- In 1967 Kechin Wang became the first Chinese Canadian to be appointed as Queen's Counsel; he was made a provincial court judge in 1971.
- Wailan Low was the first Chinese Canadian appointed to the Superior Court of Justice.

These Canadians have set a shining example; the future looks equally bright as the quest for excellence is fostered in Chinese-Canadian youth.

Young people are asking the right questions and acting on issues that negatively affect the Chinese community and the community at large. The Chinese Canadian National Council and its Toronto chapter, for example, engage young people in projects to tackle tough issues and to promote their leadership in the Chinese community.

The 15th Jean Lumb Awards 2012

林黃亦珍獎

For High School Students of Chinese Heritage
Deadline: May 28, 2012. Apply Now!
Five Award Categories, valued at $1,000 each.
Academics • Athletics • Arts • Community Services • Innovation
www.jeanlumbfoundation.ca

2011 AWARD WINNERS:
Ike Chang, Victoria Park C.I.
Clement Chao, University of Toronto Schools
Bethany So, Agincourt C.I.
Dennis Wong, Nelson H.S., Burlington
Carol Xiong, Northern S.S.

Jean Lumb Foundation.

Young people of Chinese heritage are annually recognized by organizations such as the Jean Lumb Foundation, the Chinese Cultural Centre of Greater Toronto, and the Mon Sheong Foundation.

The Native Youth Sexual Health Network, the first and only organization of its kind for First Nations youth, was founded in 2006 by Scarborough-born Jessica Yee, who describes herself as a "multiracial Indigenous hip-hop feminist reproductive justice freedom fighter."[6]

Gorick Ng, who is currently studying at Harvard University, served as a student trustee with the Toronto District School Board, president of the Ontario Student Trustee Association, head of student council at Marc Garneau Collegiate, and student ambassador for the Toronto Foundation for Student Success. He was named one of *Time* magazine's top twenty-five future leaders from around the world.

Exceptional young people such as these continue where past generations have left off and ensure that the foundation, paved with the perseverance and resilience of the early Chinese, will not crumble.

There are many other accomplished Chinese Canadians from Toronto — some have been acknowledged in the preceding chapters, but there are many others, too numerous to recognize on these pages. Their important contributions, not only to life in Toronto but to life in Canada, give us many reasons to admire their courage and determination. Many have been recognized with the Order of Canada and the Order of Ontario (see Appendices A and B). The list continues to grow.

• • •

Conclusion

More than one million Chinese Canadians live in this country. After English and French, the two official languages, Chinese is the third most spoken language, with two-thirds of its speakers using Cantonese (Yue), one-third Mandarin, and a smaller proportion speaking Hakka, Hokkien-Taiwanese (Minnan), Shanghainese (Wu), and other dialects.

Most Canadians of Chinese heritage (74.5 percent) were born outside of Canada. China supplies the most Chinese immigrants, followed by Hong Kong, Taiwan, and Vietnam (see Table 6). In 2006 China was the top source of all newcomers to Canada.

• • •

TABLE 6: Source of Foreign-born Chinese Living in Canada

Origin	Percentage of Chinese Canadians who are Foreign-born
China	52.9
Hong Kong	24.2
Taiwan	7.4
Vietnam	5.7

Source: Census 2006.

• • •

The old Huron word To'ron'to means "a place of meeting," and also suggests "a gateway" and "a place of many people." Toronto means all these things. It's been a gateway to a good life and a place for many immigrants who came from distant lands. With more than 175 years of history, Toronto has been shaped by diverse ethnic and racial groups from around the world. In the early years, 80 percent were English, Scottish, and Irish, some arriving from Britain, others from the United States. Toronto was a very British city until Canada opened its doors to the world after World War Two.

Today 47 percent of its people are visible minorities; the population is made up of two hundred distinct ethnic groups who speak over 140 languages and dialects. The Chinese population is 283,075, 11 percent of the city's population.[7] The Greater Toronto Area, including the City of Toronto and the surrounding regions of Peel, Halton, Durham, and York, has Canada's largest population of people who claim Chinese ancestry: 486,330.

There are Chinese-Canadian newspapers, radio stations, television stations, and magazines. Food, fashion, art, and literature have all been enriched in countless ways by the contributions of artists, writers, and journalists. Interest in Chinese-Canadian history is growing, with more information that has been incorporated into courses at high schools, colleges, and universities, as well as published in books, newspapers, magazines, and on the Internet. In 2012 the University of Toronto was the first in Canada to offer an academic program in Asian Canadian Studies.

The Chinese community has changed in the past fifty years, with Chinese arriving from diverse countries over different times and for varying reasons — all with their unique heritage, traditions, and culture. Newcomers from Hong Kong and Taiwan typically bring a wealth of education, experience, and skills. Newcomers from China are no longer coming from Guangdong but from other provinces in the south, west, north, and east. Thousands of Chinese have moved here from Vietnam, Jamaica, and other countries.

Some arrive with their families or join family members already here. Some are skilled professionals who fill hi-tech jobs in Markham and Richmond Hill. Others are unskilled workers who find lower-paying jobs in factories or restaurants. Regardless of where they live and work, Chinatown, whether it is in downtown Toronto or the ethnoburbs, provides a place where they can understand the language, celebrate their culture, go to church, buy groceries, and eat at favourite restaurants.

For non-Chinese, Chinatown is not the mysterious place that it used to be, and their interest in learning about Chinese culture and history has certainly been sparked by the rise of China as a world power.

We live in a global community. People move to Toronto and Torontonians live elsewhere. Asians marry Latinos. Europeans are neighbours with Africans. Buddhism and Islam are welcomed. Until recently, the idea of distinct and separate races was the reality. Today more and more people, through intermarriage, have genes from many different ethnic and racial groups, and the once distinct lines between East and West are blurring. More and more Chinese are joining and participating in organizations outside the Chinese community. As Ping Tan, the former president of the Toronto Chinese Business Association, stated, "To have a meaningful integration, you have to have participation."[8] An ancient Chinese saying sums it all up: "Within the four seas, all men are brothers." It is a small world after all.

Of course there continue to be problems, as is perhaps natural in a growing city with such diversity. Although the richness and complexity of so many cultures and races are sources of strength, the city faces no small challenges. Complaints are heard about the lack of equal opportunity. Studies show that East Asians are not well represented in management levels of professions such as science and engineering even though they make up a large portion of the workforce. There are still pervasive stereotypes of male and female Asians. The exploitation of newcomer workers can be found in stores, restaurants, and garment factories. Asian fishermen have been attacked on Lake Simcoe.

Incidents of anti-Chinese racism like these are sad reminders that acceptance into Canadian society can't be taken for granted. To make Canada an even better place, discrimination must be fought with the strength and determination of the pioneer Chinese immigrants. Their dream of creating the best life for themselves and their families is still the dream of all Canadians. Against all odds Chinese Canadians have survived the challenges of the past with enduring resilience, a testament to their determination to help build our nation and mine the riches of Gold Mountain.

Chinese Canadians Appointed Member of the Order of Canada, 1976–2011 (Greater Toronto Area)

Note: The Order of Canada is our country's highest civilian honour, and is awarded for lifetime achievement. There are three levels of membership: Member, Officer, and Companion.

Chinese Canadians Appointed Member of the Order of Canada, 1976–2011 (Greater Toronto Area)

1976	Jean B. Lumb
1979	Shiu Loon Kong
1987	William P. Wen
1993	Joseph Y.K. Wong
2001	Julia Chia-yi Ching
2001	Yvonne Chiu
2005	Wayson Choy
2010	Kue Young

Chinese Canadians Appointed Officer of the Order of Canada, 1976–2011 (Greater Toronto Area)

1991	Lap Chee Tsui
1992	Adrienne Clarkson
1998	Neville Poy
2000	Tak Wah Mak
2005	Alexina Louie

Chinese Canadians Appointed Companion of the Order of Canada, 1976–2011 (Greater Toronto Area)

1999	Adrienne Clarkson

Source: Governor General of Canada, "Order of Canada," The Official Website of the Governor General of Canada, *www.gg.ca/document.aspx?id=72*.

Chinese Canadians Appointed to the Order of Ontario, 1991–2011 (Greater Toronto Area)

Note: The Order of Ontario is our province's highest official honour, given to recognize individual excellence and achievement benefiting the people of Ontario or anywhere in the world.

1991	Sim Fai Liu
1996	Jeffrey Wan-shu Lo
1997	Moon Lum
1998	Lap Cheung Lee
1999	Doris Y.C. Lau
	Hin Cheung Tam
2000	Lap-Chee Tsui
2001	Alexina Louie
2002	Benson Lau
2003	Helen Lang Lu
2004	Kim Phuc Phan Thi
	Rita Tsang
2005	Hughes C. Eng
2006	Tak Wah Mak
	Albert Kai-Wing Ng
2009	Helen Chan

Source: Ontario Ministry of Citizenship and Immigration, "Order of Ontario Appointees," Official Website of the Ontario Ministry of Citizenship and Immigration, www.citizenship.gov.on.ca/english/citizenship/honours/orderofontario_appointees.shtml.

Chronology

1788	Fifty Chinese labourers build trading post in Nootka Sound
1839–1842	First Opium War
1849	California Gold Rush
1856–1860	Second Opium War
1858	Fraser River Gold Rushes
1861	Won Alexander Cumyow, first Canadian-born Chinese
1867	Birth of Canada as a nation
1871	British Columbia joins Confederation
1872	Chinese lose vote in British Columbia
1878	Sam Ching, first Chinese in Toronto
1880–1885	Construction of Canadian Pacific Railway
1885	Fifty dollar head tax imposed on Chinese immigrants
1894–1895	First Sino-Japanese War
1898	Hong Kong becomes British colony

1898–1900	Boxer Rebellion
1900	Head tax for Chinese immigrants increased to one hundred dollars
1903	Head tax increased to five hundred dollars
1911	Qing dynasty overthrown; Republic of China established
1912	Guomindang established; Ontario passes law forbidding Chinese from hiring white women
1914–1918	World War One
1916–1928	Warlord Era in China
1920	Dominion Elections Act reforms election rules in Canada; Chinese still denied right to vote
1921	Communist Party of China established
1923–1947	Chinese Exclusion Act in force

1923	Victoria Cheung, first Chinese-Canadian graduate of School of Medicine at the University of Toronto, 1st Chinese to intern at the Toronto General Hospital, and first female Chinese-Canadian doctor; Agnes Chan, first Chinese graduate of Women's College Hospital School of Nursing
1930–1939	Great Depression
1937–1945	Second Sino-Japanese War
1939–1945	World War Two
1941	Canada declares war on Japan; Japan occupies Hong Kong
1945	K. Dock Yip, 1st Chinese-Canadian lawyer
1946	Gretta (Wong) Grant, first female Chinese-Canadian lawyer
1947	Canadian Citizenship Act; Chinese Canadians gain right to vote
1948	Universal Declaration of Human Rights
1949	People's Republic of China founded
1960	Chinese Adjustment Program
1964	Ying Hope, first Chinese Canadian elected as school trustee in Toronto
1965	New City Hall opens
1966–1976	Cultural Revolution
1967	Canada is one hundred years old; universal immigration policy based on point system introduced; Kechin Wang, first Chinese Canadian appointed Queen's Counsel
1970	Canada establishes diplomatic relations with China
1971	United Nations admits China and unseats Taiwan; Kechin Wang, first Chinese Canadian appointed as Ontario court judge
1975	Vietnam War ends; Mon Sheong, Ontario's first Chinese seniors' home opens
1976	Mao Zedong dies; China introduces economic reforms; Jean Lumb, first Chinese-Canadian woman to receive the Order of Canada
1979	W5 television segment "Campus Giveaway"
1980	First official recognition by Parliament of the Chinese railway workers
1983	125th anniversary of Chinese settlement in Canada
1984	Britain signs agreement to return Hong Kong to China in 1997; Dragon Centre in Scarborough, first Asian-themed mall in North America, opens

1985	China opens door for migration
1986	New immigration incentives for investors
1987	Robert (Bob) Wong, first Ontario cabinet minister of Chinese descent
1988	Chan Han Goh, first Asian ballet dancer in National Ballet of Canada
1989	Tiananmen Square student demonstrations
1991	Sim Fai Liu, first Chinese Canadian to receive Order of Ontario; Olivia Chow, first Asian-Canadian woman elected in Toronto city council; Susan Eng, first Chinese Canadian to chair Metropolitan Toronto Police Services
1997	Hong Kong handover to China
1998	Chinese Cultural Centre of Greater Toronto opens; Vivienne Poy, first Asian Canadian appointed to the Senate of Canada; Wailan Low, first Chinese Canadian appointed to Superior Court of Justice
1999	Adrienne Clarkson, first Asian-Canadian Governor General of Canada
2006	Official government apology for head tax and Chinese Exclusion Act

2010	125th anniversary of completion of Canadian Pacific Railway
2012	University of Toronto creates a Minor in Asian Canadian Studies, the first such academic program offered by a Canadian university

Notes

Chapter 1

1. Chinese Canadian National Council, "Chinese Canadian History," CCNC. ca, *www.ccnc.ca/toronto/history/info/content.html*.

2. Wai-man Lee, *Portraits of a Challenge: An Illustrated History of the Chinese Canadians* (Toronto: Council of Chinese Canadians in Ontario, 1984), 26.

3. Richard Thomas Wright, *In a Strange Land: A Pictorial Record of the Chinese in Canada, 1788–1923* (Saskatoon: Western Producer Prairie Books, 1988), 23.

4. Ban Seng Hoe, *Beyond the Golden Mountain: Chinese Cultural Traditions in Canada* (Hull, QC: Canadian Museum of Civilization, 2003), 9.

5. Lee, *Portraits*, 64.

6. *Ibid.*, 62.

7. Wright, *In a Strange Land*, 77.

8. Evelyn Huang, with Lawrence Jeffery, *Chinese Canadians: Voices From a Community* (Vancouver: Douglas & McIntyre, 1992), 14.

9. Wright, *In a Strange Land*, 42.

10. *Ibid.*

11. Julia Ningyu Li, *Canadian Steel, Chinese Grit: A Tribute to the Chinese Who Worked on Canada's Railroads More Than a Century Ago* (Toronto: Paxlink Communications, 2000), 49.

12. Robert Amos and Kilseasa Wong, *Inside Chinatown: Ancient Culture in a New World* (Victoria, B.C.: Touchwood, 2009), 10.

13. Wright, *In a Strange Land*, 24.

14. *Port Moody Gazette* (Port Moody, B.C.), October 24, 1885.

15. William Lyon Mackenzie King, *Report by W.L. Mackenzie King, C.M.G., Deputy Minister of Labour, on the Need for the*

Suppression of the Opium Trade in Canada (Ottawa: Department of Labour, 1908).

16. Multicultural History Society of Ontario, "The Ties That Bind," MHSO.ca, *www.mhso.ca/tiesthatbind*.

17. Maureen Murray, "Success Follows Hardship," *Toronto Star*, December 26, 1999, A1.

Chapter 2

1. George Heron, *Child of the Great Depression* (Toronto: Select Press, 2005), 86.

2. Ban Seng Hoe, *Enduring Hardship: The Chinese Laundry in Canada* (Hull, QC: Canadian Museum of Civilization, 2003), 20.

3. Heron, *Child*, 87.

Chapter 3

1. Statistics Canada, *Census of Canada* (Ottawa: King's Printer, 1941).

2. George Heron, *Child of the Great Depression* (Toronto: Select Press, 2005), 85.

3. Tom MacInnes, *Oriental Occupation of British Columbia* (Vancouver: Sun Publishing Company Ltd., 1927), 13.

4. Richard Henry Thompson, "The State and the Ethnic Community" (Ph.D. thesis, University of Michigan, 1979), 102.

5. Heather Harris, and Mary Sun, *The Chinese Canadians* (Scarborough, ON: Nelson Canada, 1982), 48.

6. Chuck C.C. Wong, "The Wong Family Name" (Toronto: Wong's National Convention, 2011), 1.

7. Robert Amos and Kilseasa Wong, *Inside Chinatown: Ancient Culture in a New World* (Victoria, B.C.: Touchwood, 2009), 44.

8. Evelyn Huang, with Lawrence Jeffery, *Chinese Canadians: Voices From a Community* (Vancouver: Douglas & McIntyre, 1992), 17.

9. Sandro Contentat, "Toronto Catholic archdiocese a multi-million organization in transition," *Toronto Star*, February 11, 2012.

10. Sol Littman, "Growing Up Chinese in Metro Toronto," *Toronto Star*, April 5, 1981, D5.

11. Chinese Canadian National Council, Women's Book Committee, *Jin Guo* (Toronto: Women's Press, 1992), 158.

12. Littman, "Growing Up Chinese."

13. Huang, with Jeffery, *Chinese Canadians*, 19.

Chapter 4

1. Multicultural History Society of Ontario, "The Ties That Bind," MHSO.ca, *www.mhso.ca/tiesthatbind*.

2. Chinese Canadian National Council, Women's Book Committee. *Jin Guo* (Toronto: Women's Press, 1992), 172.

Chapter 5

1. Richard Thomas Wright, *In a Strange Land: A Pictorial Record of the Chinese in Canada, 1788–1923* (Saskatoon: Western Producer Prairie Books, 1988), 104.

2. Jonathan Webb, *Canada's Wars: An Illustrated History* (Toronto: Madison Press Books, 2010), 41.

3. Adrian Ma, *How the Chinese Created Canada* (Edmonton: Dragon Hill Publishing Ltd.), 70.

4. Robert Wong, "Building an Aeroplane in Vancouver's Chinatown," Unpublished manuscript, circa 1980.

Chapter 6

1. Wai-Man Lee, "Lee Chang," in *Portraits of a Challenge: An Illustrated History of the Chinese Canadians* (Toronto: Council of Chinese Canadians in Ontario, 1984), 186.

2. Multicultural History Society of Ontario, "Chinese Canadian Women, 1923–1967," MHSO.ca, *www.mhso.ca/ chinesecanadianwomen/en/*.

3. Citizens for Public Justice, "The Head Tax and Its Early History," CPJ.ca, *www. cpj.ca/files/docs/headtax_kit_no_cover1.pdf*.

4. Chinese Canadian National Council, Women's Book Committee. *Jin Guo* (Toronto: Women's Press, 1992), 55.

5. Philip Marchand, "Toronto Chinese," in William Kilbourn, *Toronto Remembered: A Celebration of the City* (Toronto: Stoddart, 1984), 235.

6. Edward Keenan, "Vivienne Poy Makes Waves from Hong Kong to Canada's Senate," canadianimmigrant.ca, *http://canadianimmigrant.ca/immigrant-stories/vivienne-poy-makes-waves-from-hong-kong-to-canadas-senate*.

7. Maynard Parker, "Reports: Hong Kong," *The Atlantic Monthly*, November, 1967, 26.

8. *Frontline*, "The Tank Man," PBS.org, *www.pbs.org/wgbh/pages/frontline/tank-man/interviews/wong.html*.

9. Peter Li, *The Chinese in Canada* (Toronto: Oxford University Press, 1988), 91.

10. Multicultural History Society of Ontario, "The Safe Haven Exhibition," MHSO.ca, *www.mhso.ca/ggp/Exhibits//Safe_Haven/ about.html*.

11. Julia Turner, "From Pirate Raids to Ontario Winter," *Globe and Mail*, December 20, 1979, 5.

12. Susan Hughes, *Coming to Canada* (Toronto: Maple Tree Press, 2005), 96.

13. Hughes, *Coming to Canada*, 104.

14. Statistics Canada, *Census of Canada* (Ottawa: Queen's Printer, 2006).

Chapter 7

1. Claire Mackay, *The Toronto Story* (Toronto: Annick Press, 2002), 123.

2. Nicholas Keung, "Rag Trade's Hidden Hands: Women Afraid to Complain Finally Find a Voice," *Toronto Star*, October 28, 2005, B1.

3. Statistics Canada, *Census of Canada* (Ottawa: Queen's Printer, 2006).

4. Sandro Contenta and Jim Rankin, "In Markham, Ethnic Enclave 'Is Heaven,'" *Toronto Star*, July 1, 2012, A1.

Chapter 8

1. Wai-Man Lee, *Portraits of a Challenge: An Illustrated History of the Chinese Canadians* (Toronto: Council of Chinese Canadians in Ontario, 1984), 180.

2. Anthony B. Chan, *Gold Mountain: The Chinese in the New World* (Vancouver: New Star Books, 1983), 165.

3. Office of the Prime Minister of Canada, "Prime Minister Harper Offers Full Apology for the Chinese Head Tax," pm.gc. ca, *www.pm.gc.ca/eng/media.asp?id=1219*.

4. Paul Yee, *Struggle and Hope: The Story of Chinese Canadians* (Toronto: Umbrella Press, 1996), 60.

5. Nicholas Keung, "The Painful Choice of 'Satellite Babies,'" *Toronto Star*, May 11, 2009, GT1.

6. Government of Canada, "Adoption," China.gc.ca, *www.canadainternational. gc.ca/china-chine/visas/intl_adoption_itl. aspx?view=d*.

7. Chinese Canadian National Council, Women's Book Committee, *Jin Guo* (Toronto: Women's Press, 1992), 174.

8. *Ibid.*, 53.

9. Evelyn Huang, with Lawrence Jeffery, *Chinese Canadians: Voices From a Community* (Vancouver: Douglas & McIntyre, 1992), 251.

10. A. Ka Tat Tsang et al., "Negotiating Ethnic Identity in Canada: The Case of the Satellite Children," *Youth & Society* 34, no. 3 (March 2003): 371.

11. Chinese Canadian National Council, *Jin Guo*, 54.

12. *Ibid.*, 66.

13. Katherine Barber, "Quick and Nimble Chopsticks," *Toronto Star*, February 19, 2010, L4.

Chapter 9

1. Wynne Parry, "Teen Discovers Promising Cystic Fibrosis Treatment," *LiveScience Writer*, May 12, 2011 (*www.livescience. com/14138-teen-cystic-fibrosis-drug-cock-tail-contest.html*).

2. Brian C. Zhang, "After Degrassi, Harvard," *The Harvard Crimson*, November 30, 2011 (*www.thecrimson.com/article/2011/11/30/ judy_jiao_degrassi_harvard/*).

3. Dennis Iversson, "Scott Pilgrim vs. Ellen Wong," *Movie Maker*, August 13, 2010 (*www.moviemaker.com/arti-cles-acting/ellen-wong-scott-pilgrim-vs-the-world-20100813/*).

4. Asia/Canada, *www.histori.ca/asia-canada/ page.do?subclassN=IssuepageID=353*.

5. Edward Keenan, "Vivienne Poy Makes Waves from Hong Kong to Canada's Senate," canadianimmigrant.ca, *http:// canadianimmigrant.ca/immigrant-stories/ vivienne-poy-makes-waves-from-hong-kong-to-canadas-senate*.

6. Native Youth Sexual Health Network, *www.nativeyouthsexualhealth.com/execu-tivedirector.html*.

7. Statistics Canada, *Census of Canada* (Ottawa: Queen's Printer, 2006).

8. Craig MacInnis, "Chinese Toronto: The Best of Both Worlds," *Toronto Star*, February 7, 1986, D19.

Glossary

Amnesty: A general pardon issued by the government for past offences.

Ancestors: People from the past who are related.

Bachelor: An unmarried man.

Buddha: The name given to Siddhartha Gautama (circa 563–483 BCE), a nobleman and religious teacher who devoted his life to seeking spiritual enlightenment.

Buddhism: The teachings of Buddha and his followers who spread the word of enlightenment and peace. It is one of China's main religions and the world's fourth largest, with 360 million followers.

Canadian Victory Bond: Certificates sold by the Canadian government to help pay for World War One and Two.

Cantonese: Chinese dialect spoken mostly in Guangdong province, Hong Kong, and Macau; also refers to the people and style of Chinese cooking from Guangdong.

Chinese Nationalist League: *See* Guomindang.

Civil War: The war between people or groups from different regions of the same country.

Cold War: A state of political tension and military rivalry between nations, particularly the United States and Soviet Union after World War Two.

Communism: A political system that strives for a classless society where private property is banned and industry and farming are owned collectively by the people.

Confucianism: A philosophy based on the teachings of Confucius. His teachings exercised a major influence on the political, social, and cultural life of China.

Confucius: A Chinese philosopher (551–479) who was a great teacher of morals.

Culture: The customs, traditions, and values of a country or its people.

Daoism: A philosophy based on the teachings of Laozi. It promotes a simple life that fits into the natural flow of events.

Democracy: A government by the people, exercised either directly or through elected representatives.

Dialect: A form of language spoken in a particular region or group. There are hundreds of dialects in China, such as Cantonese and Hakka.

Dynasty: A historical period of rulers from the same family.

Emigrate: To leave one country to settle in another.

Gold Mountain: The Chinese term for North America.

Gold rush: Sudden migration of people to an area where gold has been found

Great Depression: A time between 1929 and 1939 when Canada and the rest of the world experienced a long-term downturn in economic activity.

Gum Shan: *See* Gold Mountain.

Guomindang: A political party founded by Sun Yat-sen in 1912. Also known as the Nationalist Party and in Canada as the Chinese Nationalist League.

Han: The main ethnic group in China.

Head tax: A fixed fee charged for each Chinese person entering Canada.

Heritage: Traditions passed down to younger generations.

Immigrants: Newcomers to a country.

Immigrate: To enter and settle in a country or region to which one is not native.

Kuomintang: *See* Guomindang

Mainstream: The values and traditions of the majority.

Manchus: The people who came from Manchuria and established the Qing (or Manchu) dynasty (1644–1911).

Mandarin: The official language of China.

Matchmaker: Someone who arranges marriages.

Middle class: A social, economic, and cultural grouping usually composed of business, professional, and skilled people; between the upper class and the lower class.

Nationalist Party: *See* Guomindang.

Paper son: A young Chinese male who entered Canada with identity papers that were bought for him. The same practice was used for females, who were called paper daughters.

Pinyin: A system of spelling used to translate Chinese characters into the Latin alphabet so that they can be read by speakers of European languages, such as English.

Prospector: A person who searches for gold or other precious metals.

Qi: The vital energy believed to circulate around the body in currents, or meridians.

Racism: Discrimination or prejudice against a person or group based on racial, ethnic, or cultural differences.

Red Scare: A time period of general fear of Communists and Communism.

Refugees: People who leave a country for fear of persecution based on race, ethnicity, religion, political opinion, sexual orientation, or nationality.

Revolution: A significant change, including the overthrow of a governing regime.

Segregation: The policy or practice of separating people of different races, classes, or ethnic groups, especially as a form of discrimination.

Suburb: The residential region around a major city.

Traditional Chinese medicine: A healing tradition of ancient China, based on the manipulation of the body's qi or natural energy.

Traditions: The cultural rituals, customs, and practices of a particular country, people, family, or institution handed down over a long period of time.

Values: Beliefs that are considered important by an individual or a culture.

Visible minority: Someone who is not First Nations or Caucasian, i.e., white.

Warlord: A person with power who has both military and civil control over an area and its population due to his leadership of armed forces.

Yin and yang: These are the terms given to the twin and opposing natures that traditional Chinese culture believes exist in the world. They are complementary and balance each other. Yin refers to things that are dark, cold, wet, and feminine. Yang refers to bright, hot, dry, and masculine things.

Further Reading

Amos, Robert, and Kilseasa Wong. *Inside Chinatown: Ancient Culture in a New World*. Victoria, B.C.: Touchwood, 2009.

Chan, Gillian. *An Ocean Apart: The Gold Mountain Diary of Chin Mei-ling*. Markham, ON: Scholastic Canada, 2004.

Chinese Canadian National Council, Women's Book Committee. *Jin Guo: Voices of Chinese Canadian Women*. Toronto: Women's Press, 1992.

City of Toronto Archives. "Local Chinese History at the City of Toronto." In *Research Guide* 13. Toronto: City of Toronto Archives, 2009.

Harris, Heather, and Mary Sun. *The Chinese Canadians*. Scarborough, ON: Nelson Canada, 1982.

Heron, George. *Child of the Great Depression*. Toronto: Select Press, 2005.

Hoe, Ban Seng. *Beyond the Golden Mountain: Chinese Cultural Traditions in Canada*. Hull, QC: Canadian Museum of Civilization, 1989.

———. *Enduring Hardship: The Chinese Laundry in Canada.* Hull, QC: Canadian Museum of Civilization, 2003.

Huang, Evelyn, with Lawrence Jeffery. *Chinese Canadians: Voices From a Community.* Vancouver: Douglas & McIntyre, 1992.

Hughes, Susan. *Coming to Canada: Building a Life in a New Land.* Toronto: Maple Tree Press, 2005.

Lee, Wai-Man. *Portraits of a Challenge: An Illustrated History of the Chinese Canadians.* Toronto: Council of Chinese Canadians in Ontario, 1984.

Mackay, Claire. *The Toronto Story.* Toronto: Annick Press, 2002.

Stepanchuk, Carol. *Exploring Chinatown: A Children's Guide to Chinese Culture.* Berkeley, CA: Pacific View Press, 2002.

Webb, Jonathan. *Canada's Wars: An Illustrated History.* Toronto: Madison Press Books, 2010.

Welldon, Christine. *Canadian Pacific Railway: Pong Git Cheng.* Toronto: Grolier Ltd., 1991.

Wright, Richard Thomas. *In a Strange Land: A Pictorial Record of the Chinese in Canada, 1788–1923.* Saskatoon: Western Producer Prairie Books, 1988.

Yee, Paul. *Chinatown: An Illustrated History of the Chinese Communities of Victoria, Vancouver, Calgary, Winnipeg, Toronto, Ottawa, Montreal and Halifax.* Toronto: James Lorimer, 2005.

———. *Struggle and Hope: The Story of Chinese Canadians.* Toronto: Umbrella Press, 1996.

Web Sites

Li, Peter S. "Chinese." In *Encyclopedia of Canada's Peoples*, edited by Paul R. Magocsi. Toronto: Multicultural History Society of Ontario; University of Toronto Press, 1999. Accessed via Multicultural Canada, "Chinese," Multiculturalcanada.ca. *http://multiculturalcanada. ca/Encyclopedia/A-Z/c10*.

Library and Archives Canada. "Across the Generations: A History of the Chinese in Canada." Canada's Digital Collections. *www.collectionscanada.gc.ca/eppp-archive/100/205/301/ic/cdc/ generations/index2.html*.

Library and Archives Canada. "The Early Chinese Canadians, 1858–1947." Collectionscanada. gc.ca. *www.collectionscanada.gc.ca/chinese-canadians/021022-1200-e.html*.

Multicultural History Society of Ontario. "Chinese Canadian Women, 1923–1967." MHSO. ca. *www.mhso.ca/chinesecanadianwomen/en*.

Multicultural History Society of Ontario. "The Ties That Bind." MHSO.ca. *www.mhso.ca/ tiesthatbind/*.

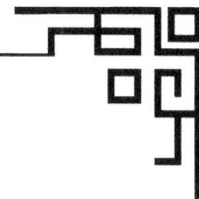

Index

Numbers in italics refer to images and their captions.

adoption, 126
Agincourt, *see* Scarborough
ancestors, 50, 51, 54, 55, 132
anti-Chinese discrimination, *see* discrimination
Asian Heritage Month, 146
associations, 48–50, 51, 53, 62, 108
"astronauts," 125

bachelor society, 101, 121
Bates, Judy Fong, 142
boat people, 99, 100, 123
Borden, Robert, 73
Boxer Rebellion, 52
Britain, 28, 51, 52, 71, 72, 76, 79, 86, 91, 95, 97, 98, 137, 150
British Columbia, 11, 16, 19, 22, 24, 25, 26, 32, 34, 35, 57, 71, 72, 79, 86, 89, 141, 146
Buddhism, 55, 151

burials, 50

cafés, *see* restaurants
Cambodia, 99
"Campus Giveaway," see W5
Canada, 12, 14, 19–20, *21*, 22, 23, 24, *25*, 26, 28, 29, *31*, 32, 33, 35, 41, 43, 44, 45, 48, 49, 52, 53, 62, 64, 70, 71, 72, 73, 74, 76, 78, 79, 82, 83, 85, 86, 87, 88, 89, 91, 92, 94, 95–96, 97, 98–99, 100, 101, 102, 112, 114, 116, 120, 122, 123, 124, 125, 126, 127, 128, 133, 134, 138, 139–40, 141, 142, 143, 144, 146, 148, 149, 150, 151, 152
Canadian-born Chinese, 66, 125, 128
Canadian Pacific Railway (CPR), 13–22, *23*, 24–29, 63, 143
Cantonese, *see* Chinese language
Chan, Agnes, 57

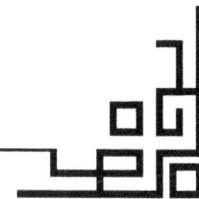

Chan, Han Goh, 148

Chan, Jackie, 59

Chan, Ka Nin, *143*

Chan, Michael, 147

Chan, Patrick, 140, *141*

Chan, Paul, 134

Chang, G. Raymond, 148

Cheung, Charlie, 111–12

Cheung, Victoria, 57

Chiang Kai-shek, 74, 75, 76, 100

children, 13, *44*, 46, 59, 62, 63, 64, 65, 66–68, 69, 70, 78, 82, 85, 86, 87, 88–89, 90, 91, 99, 101, 102, *104*, 107, 108, 125, 126, 128, 132, 142, 146

China, 11, 12, 13–14, *15*, 16, 19–20, 26, 28, 29, 45–46, 47, 48, 49–50, 51, 52, 53, 55, 57, 62, 64, 71, 72, *73*, 74, *75*, 76, 79, 80, 85, 87, 88, 91, 92–93, 94, 95, 96, 97, 98, 100, 101, 102, 107, 112, 114, 116, 118, 119–20, 125, 126, 129, 130, 131, 132, 134, 137, 142, 144, 150, 151, *see also* People's Republic of China, Republic of China

Chinatown, 11, 12, 35, *37*, 38, 42, *43*, 44, 45, 46, 48, 49, *50*, *53*, 56, 57, 60, 63, 64, 66, *67*, 75, 80, 82, 83, 88, 89, 95, 103, *105*, 106, 109, *110*, *111*, *112*, *113*, 122, 127, 134, 137, 138, 145, 146, 147, 151, *see also* ethnoburbs, Markham, Mississauga, Richmond Hill, Scarborough

Chinatown, Old, 106, 111, 116, 145

Chinatown East, *53*, 111, *112*, *113*, 116

Chinatown West, *50*, *56*, 106, 107, 108, 109, *110*, *111*, 116, 121, *122*, 133–34, 147

Chinese Canadian National Council, 124, 145, 148

Chinese Canadians, 12, 49, 61, 62, 79, 85, 86, 101, 116, 120, *122*, 124, 126–27, 128, 139, 140, 143, 145, 146, 147, 148, 149, 150, 152

Chinese Cultural Centre of Greater Toronto, *54*, 126, *133*, 134, *149*

Chinese Empire Reform Association, 52

Chinese Exclusion Act, *44*, 45, 46, 61, 76, 82–83, 85, 86, 88, 89, 95, 101, 123

Chinese Freemasons Association 52, 61, *see also* associations

Chinese Immigration Act, 44

Chinese Labour Corps, 72, *73*

Chinese language, 49–50, 57, 65, 93, 108, 118, 129, 130, 131–32, 137, 150

Chinese Nationalist League or Chinese Nationalist Party, *see* Guomindang

Chinese New Year, 132

Ching, Sam, 33, 48

Chong, Gordon, 59

Chong Ying, *81*

Chow, Dennis, *41*

Chow, Ian, 59

Chow, Olivia, 147

Choy, Wayson, 142

Chu, Philip, 61

churches, 11–12, 56–57, 62, 63, 68, 69, 76, 80, 111, 132, 151

citizenship, 86, 87

City Hall, New, 33, 103, *104*

City Hall, Old, *33*

civil war, 51, 52, 74, 92, 94, 96, 99

Clarkson, Adrienne, 146

Cold War, 91–92

communism, 75, 92, 96, 99

Confucius, 53, *54*

county associations, 48–49

CPR, *see* Canadian Pacific Railway

Cultural Revolution, 94

Cumyow, Won Alexander, 49

Daoism, 54–55

Deng Xiaoping, 102

Depression, 11, 25, 42, 62, 71, 76, 89

Diefenbaker, John, *90*

discrimination, 26, 28, 39, 56, 67, 139, 152

Dominion Elections Act, 74

Dragon Boat Festival, 132–33

Dragon Centre, 116, *117*

Dragon City, *109*

education, *see* schools

Eng, Sam, 20, 53, 62

Eng, Susan, 148

ethnic minority groups, 13, 120, 145

ethnoburbs, 114, 117–18, 151

family, 12, 13, 26, 29, *31*, 46, 48, 49, 50, 54, 60, 62, 63, 66, 67, 70, 82, 86, 88–89, 90–91, 95, 97, 100, 101, 106, 125, 126, 132, 134, 137, 142, 151

family associations, 12, 48–49, 108

food, 14, 16, 29, 37, 42, 43, 45, 46, 50, 52, 62, 63, 72, 78, 96, 106, 108, 109, *112*, 120, 132, 137, 138, 150

France, 28, 52, 71, 72, *73*, 76, 79, 82, 91, 146

franchise, *see* vote

Fu-GEN Asian Canadian Theatre Company, 143–44

garment workers, 107, 145

Germany, 26, 28, 33, 52, 71, 74, 76, 79, 92

Go, Avvy, 145

Goh, Chan Hon, 148

Gold Mountain (Gum Shan), 16, 19, 46, 47, 142, 152

gold rush, 16, 17

Grant, Gretta (Wong), 128, 146

Great Depression, *see* Depression

Greater Toronto Area (GTA), 57, 116, *121*, 125, 133, 134, 137, 147, 150

Guangdong, 11, 14, *15*, 20, 94, 131, 151

Guomindang, 53, 74, 92

Han dynasty, 13
Harper, Stephen, 124
head tax, 11, 28–29, *30*, *31*, 32, 43, 45, 64, 89, 95, 124–25, 144–45
Head Tax Campaign, 124–25, 145
Ho, Alice Ping Yee, 143
Ho, Matthew, 140
Hong Kong, 28, 51, 78, 79, 80, 88, 91, 94, 95, 96–98, 100, 102, 106, 111, 113, 116, 120, 125, 126, 130, 132, 146, 150, 151
Hong Luck Kung Fu Club, 134
Hope, Ying, 148
Hum, Fern, 127

immigration, 29, 32, 44, 45, 49, 73, 83, 89, 90, 91, 95, 96, 100, 101
Indochina, 99–100
Ing, Eddie, 95

Japan, 75–76, 78, 79, 80, 92, 96, 97, 101
Jiao, Judy, 144
Jing Mo Kung Fu Club, 134
Jung, Douglas, 146

Keung, Chow, 41
King, William Lyon Mackenzie, 79
kung fu, 123, 134, 135

Kuomintang, *see* Guomindang
Kwan, Cheuk, 49, 145, 147
Kwong Hoi Hui Kuan, 49

Lam, Vincent, 142
language, *see* Chinese language
Laos, 99
Laozi, 54
laundries, 32, 33, 39, *41*, 43, 48, 66, 106
Lee, Bruce, 134
Lee, Sook-Yin, 143
Lee-Chin, Michael, 148
Lem Si Ho Tong (Lem Society), 49
Li She Kong So (Lee Association), 49
Lightfoot, Gordon, 24
literacy, 130, 131
Lock, Joan, 82, 83
Lock, Keith, 144
Lock, Quong, 45
Lock, Tom (George Thomas), 82, *83*
Lore, Henry, 60, 61, 88
Lore, Jimmy, 134
Louie, Alexina, 143
Low, Wailan, 148
Lumb, Doyle, 11, 32
Lumb, Jean, 11, *45*, 89, 90, 103, 127–28, 145, *149*
Lung Kong Kung So, 49, 108

Macau, 14, 28, 91, 130
Macdonald, John A., 19
Mah, Valerie, 60
Mak, Tak Wah, 139
Manchu dynasty, 52, 53, 70, 74
Mandarin, *see* Chinese language
Mao Zedong, 74, 76, 92, 93, 94, 102
Mark, Dak Leon, 124, 125
Mark, E.C., *81*
Markham, 57, *115*, *117*, 119, 120, *122*, 140, 147, 151
martial arts, 58, 134, *135*, 137
Meares, John, 14
media, 19, *39*, 73, 146
medicine, 24, 29, 57, 60, 61, 106, 123
Memorial to Commemorate the Chinese Railroad Workers, *25*
Mid-Autumn Festival, 133
Ming dynasty, 28
missionaries, 56
Mississauga, *115*, *117*, 118, 119, *122*
Mississauga Chinese Centre, 118
Mon Sheong Foundation, 122, 132, *149*
music, 13, 57, 58, 69–70, 76, 80, 132, 134, 141–42, 143

names, 47–48, 49, 91, 130
Nationalist Party, *see* Guomindang
Ng, Gorick, 149
Ng, Winnie, 145
Nipp, Dora, 145
North York, 114, 117, 140

Onderdonk, Andrew, 19, 26
one-child policy, 102, 126
opera, 57, 58, *59*, 60, 76, 132, 143
Operation Oblivion, 79
Opium Wars, 28, 51

Pacific Mall, 120, *121*
paper sons and daughters, 90–91
People's Republic of China, 92, 93, 96, 101
Pinyin, 130
political associations, 51
Pon, James, 64
Poy, Neville, 139
Poy, Vivienne, 97, 146, *147*
Pure Brightness Festival, 132

Quan, Donald, 143
Queen Victoria, 28
Qing dynasty, 28, 51, 52, 53

racism, *see* discrimination
railway and railway workers, *see* Canadian Pacific Railway
reading, *see* Chinese language
Reeves, Keanu, 144

refugees, *see* Indochina, Hong Kong, People's Republic of China.
religious life, 54, 57, 96
Republic of China, 53, 92, 93, 100
restaurants, 32, 38, 42, *43*, 44, 56, 66, 96, 106, 108, 109, 113, 114, 116, 120, 137, 145, 151, 152
Richmond Hill, *115*, *117*, 119–20, *122*, 129, 140, 146, 151
Rowswell, Mark, 129
Royal Commission, 29
Russia, 26, 28, 32, 35, 45, 52, 71

Scarborough, 114, *115*, 116, *117*, 119, 120, *122*, *133*, 141, 144, 147, 149
schools, 11–12, 46, 52, 58, 66, 111, 123, 126, 132, 134, 144, 151
Shih, Hsio Yen, 148
Sino-Japanese War, 71, 74, 75–76, 96
Smith, Donald Alexander, 24
Southern Legs Northern Fists, *135*
Soviet Union, 91, 92
Spadina Expressway, 108
Special Forces Unit, 82
sports, 68, 133, 140
Spring Festival, 132
Starlight Chinese Opera, 58
Stojko, Elvis, 134
Sun Yat-sen, 52, 53

sweatshops, 107

Tai chi, 137
Taishanese, *see* Chinese language
Taiwan, *see* Republic of China
Tan, Ping, 151
Tang, Sunny, 134
Tang dynasty, 35
temples, *55*, 94
Tiananmen Square, 98, 100
Toronto Chinese Business Association, 132, 151
traditional Chinese medicine, 60
Tran, Timothy, 100
Trudeau, Pierre Elliott, 96, 101
Tsui, Lap Chee, 139

United Nations, 83–84, 85, 92–93, 99, 100
United States, 19, 74, 78, 85, 91, 92, 95, 97, 100, 101, 150

Vancouver, 11, 14, *30*, 32, *43*, 57, 89, 100, 124, 142, 146
Victoria, 34–35, 43, *141*
Vietnam, 91, 92, 99–100, 108, 150, 151
vote, 71, 74, 79, 86, 144

W5, 123, 145
Wang, Kechin, 148

war brides, 82
warlords, 74–75
Ward, The, 35, 36, *37*, 38
Wilson, Woodrow, 74
Winter Solstice Festival, 134
women, 32, 45, 46, 47, 57, 69, 74, 76, 78, 79,
    82, 85, 101, 107, 108, 122
Wong, Ellen, 144
Wong, Jan, 14, 98, 142
Wong, Joseph Y.K., 145
Wong, Robert (Bob), 148
Wong, Robert and Tommy, *81*, 82
Wong, William C., 66
Wong Wun Sun King So (Wong Association),
    49, *50*
Woo, Stanley, *50*
World War One, 57, 71, 83
World War Two, 12, 64, 76, 80, 85, 91, 92,
    95, 96, 107, 134, 145, 150
writing, *see* Chinese language

Yao, Eugene, 145
Yee, Jessica, 149
Yee, Paul, *142*
Yee Hong Foundation, *122*
Yin and yang, 54, *111*
Yip, K. Dock, 146
Young, Kue, 139

Zhang, Marshall, 49, 140

BY THE SAME AUTHOR

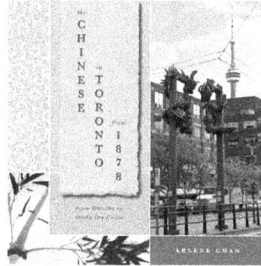

The Chinese in Toronto from 1878
From Outside to Inside the Circle
by Arlene Chan
978-1554889792
$35.00

The modest beginnings of the Chinese in Toronto and the development of Chinatown is largely due to the completion of the CPR in 1885. No longer requiring the services of the Chinese labourers, a hostile British Columbia sent them eastward in search of employment and a more welcoming place.

In 1894 Toronto's Chinese population numbered fifty. Today, no less than seven Chinatowns serve what has become the second-largest visible minority in the city, with a population of half a million. In these pages, you will find their stories told through historical accounts, archival and present-day photographs, newspaper clippings, and narratives from old-timers and newcomers. With achievements spanning all walks of life, the Chinese in Toronto are no longer looking in from outside society's circle. Their lives are a vibrant part of the diverse mosaic that makes Toronto one of the most multicultural cities in the world.

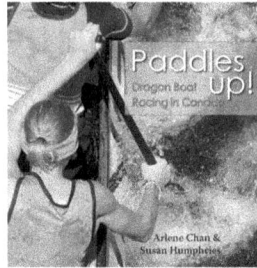

Paddles Up!
Dragon Boat Racing in Canada
by Arlene Chan
978-1554883950
$35.00

Paddles Up! provides an in-depth look at dragon boating from its beginnings in ancient China to the modern-day prominence of Canadian teams on the international scene, as told in the words of top coaches of men's and women's teams, experts and enthusiasts, and sports health professionals across Canada. Contributing writers include Mike Haslam, executive president International Dragon Boat Federation; Matthew Smith, president Dragon Boat Canada; Kamini Jain, Vancouver; Albert MacDonald, Halifax; Jamie Hollins, Pickering; Matt Robert, Montreal; and Jim Farintosh, Toronto. Through legends, history, and traditions, to paddling tips and mental readiness, and from choosing gear to exceptional achievements, a battery of Canadian dragon-boat notables share their considerable knowledge in one authoritative volume.

DUNDURN

Visit us at
Dundurn.com | Definingcanada.ca | @dundurnpress | Facebook.com/dundurnpress

www.ingramcontent.com/pod-product-compliance
Lightning Source LLC
Chambersburg PA
CBHW062042090426
42740CB00016B/2998